S n
the Storm

E.G. WHITE

A combination of the complete book
STEPS TO CHRIST
with sixty pages from
THE GREAT CONTROVERSY
plus two added introductory pages to each chapter

Should the surges rise,
And rest delay to come,
Blest be the tempest,
Kind the storm,
Which driveth us nearer home,
— from an old English poem

HB–123

Shelter in the Storm

by Ellen G. White

Published by Harvestime Books

Altamont, TN 37301 USA

Printed in the United States of America

ABOUT THE COVER—In the storms of life, we can only be safe with divine help. The storms come, fiercer than any we can imagine. But God will make a way of protection for those who will cling to Him and to His Inspired Word. The light of heaven will illuminate the path before them; His hand will guide the wheel.

The painting on the cover was prepared by the nationally known artist, John Steel, especially for this book. In describing it, Mr. Steel said: 'I left the yards off the mizzenmast, and made a bark of her. A bark had three masts: with foremast and mainmast, square rigged, and the mizzenmast (the third mast), fore and aft rigged. It was a vessel which had the features both of the square-rigger and the schooner."

This present volume is primarily composed of all or part of two books. Both have been reset in an easy-to-read large typeface that will encourage many more people to read them.

The first thirteen chapters are *STEPS TO CHRIST* (the 1892 edition), unabridged. The last five chapters (chapters 14-16) are from *GREAT CONTROVERSY* (sixty pages from the 1888 edition of this book). We added two introductory pages to each chapter.

It is widely recognized that chapters 2-3, 25, 29, and 35 are among the most important chapters in *Great Controversy*. These are the chapters that we drew most heavily upon in the preparation of the last five chapters in this present volume. (See page 203 for additional information.)

FOR ADDITIONAL COPIES —

This book may be purchased singly or in boxful quantities. Please contact the publisher for current prices.

Contents

CHAPTER ONE

God's Love for You

"It had been a foggy afternoon. I was off the Atlantic Coast in my fishing boat. I always went out alone, and had been busy working my nets.

"As evening came on, I noticed that another fishing boat was anchored nearby. I saw that he was also working alone. Although I did not know who he was, I waved and noted that he did not respond. He looked drunk. I went below deck, exhausted from the day's work and fell asleep in my clothes.

"I was too tired to take them off.

"It must have been 11 or 12 o'clock when I heard the yelling. Up on deck, I ran to the railing—and saw him in the water. Too drunk to know better, he had fallen overboard.

"The cold water had started him shouting.

"Quickly I stripped down and dove overboard. It was obvious he would be gone in another minute. How I ever got him on board his fishing boat, I'll never know. I carried him below deck, got dry clothes on him, and put him into his bunk. I made him some food, and stayed until he was warm and sleeping soundly.

"Utterly wearied from it all, I did not want to disturb him; so, instead of starting the engine, I dove back into the cold Atlantic and swam to my own boat.

I almost didn't make it. Exhausted, I fell into my bunk, but with the happy knowledge that I had saved his life. Twice I had come close to drowning that night,—but a man had been saved from drowning.

"A man I didn't know.

"Next morning broke clear and sunny. I awoke about eight, and went up on deck.

"My new friend was leaning on the rail.

" 'Hi,' I called out cheerily. 'How are you doing this morning?' With a growl, he told me to shut my mouth.

" 'But I'm your best friend!' I cried. 'I saved your life last night!' At this, he called me a liar and threw every curse word at me that he knew.

"I went below deck and put my face in my hands and wept. It was then—for the first time in my life—that I really understood the love of God in trying to save men.

For I had seen a little of what it cost Him, and what they had given Him in return. And I realized that in that love is our only hope . ."

That incident took place nearly a hundred years ago, but it points us to a deep truth that has changed lives—and can bring a deep happiness to yours.

In the chapters of this book, you will find information that for years you may have been searching for. And what you will find is not difficult. For it is the Bible path to God.

Here you will learn not only how to come to Him, but how to stay with Him in spite of life's turmoils.

And here you will find a love and a forgiveness, an encouragement and a help,—such as you may never before have thought possible.

Yes, simple steps to a better and happier life. The path home you have been looking for.

For, you see, it all began with the love of God.

Nature and revelation alike testify of God's love. Our Father in heaven is the source of life, of wisdom, and of joy. Look at the wonderful and beautiful things of nature. Think of their marvelous adaptation to the needs and happiness, not only of man, but of all living creatures. The sunshine and the rain, that gladden and refresh the earth, the hills and seas and plains, all speak to us of the Creator's love. It is God who supplies the daily needs of all His creatures. In the beautiful words of the psalmist: "The eyes of all wait upon Thee; and Thou givest them their meat in due season. Thou openest Thine hand, and satisfiest the desire of every living thing." *Psalm 145:15-16.*

God made man perfectly holy and happy; and the fair earth, as it came from the Creator's hand, bore no blight of decay or shadow of the curse. It is transgression of God's law—the law of love—that has brought woe and death. Yet even amid the suffering that results from sin, God's love is revealed. It is written that God cursed the ground for man's sake (*Genesis 3:17*). The thorn and the thistle—the difficulties and trials that make his life one of toil and care—were appointed for his good as a part of the training needful in God's plan for his uplifting from the ruin and degradation that sin has wrought. The world, though fallen, is not all sorrow and misery. In nature itself are messages of hope and comfort. There are flowers upon the thistles, and the thorns are covered with roses.

Written in Nature

"God is love" is written upon every opening bud, upon every spire of springing grass. The lovely birds making the air vocal with their happy songs, the delicately tinted flowers in their perfection perfuming the air, the lofty trees of the forest with their rich foliage of living green—all testify to the tender, fatherly care of our God and to His desire to make His children happy.

The Word of God reveals His character. He Himself has declared His infinite love and pity. When Moses prayed, "Show me Thy glory," the Lord answered, "I will make all My goodness pass before thee" (*Exodus 33:18-19*). This is

His glory. The Lord passed before Moses, and proclaimed, "The Lord, The Lord God, merciful and gracious, longsuffering, and abundant in goodness and truth, keeping mercy for thousands, forgiving iniquity and transgression and sin." *Exodus 34:6-7.* He is "slow to anger, and of great kindness" (*Jonah 4:2*) "because He delighteth in mercy" (*Micah 7:18*).

God has bound our hearts to Him by unnumbered tokens in heaven and in earth. Through the things of nature, and the deepest and tenderest earthly ties that human hearts can know, He has sought to reveal Himself to us. Yet these but imperfectly represent His love. Though all these evidences have been given, the enemy of good blinded the minds of men, so that they looked upon God with fear; they thought of Him as severe and unforgiving. Satan led men to conceive of God as a being whose chief attribute is stern justice,—one who is a severe judge, a harsh, exacting creditor. He pictured the Creator as a being who is watching with jealous eye to discern the errors and mistakes of men, that He may visit judgments upon them. It was to remove this dark shadow, by revealing to the world the infinite love of God, that Jesus came to live among men.

Revealed in His Son

The Son of God came from heaven to make manifest the Father. "No man hath seen God at any time; the only begotten Son, which is in the bosom of the Father, He hath declared Him." *John 1:18.* "Neither knoweth any man the Father, save the Son, and he to whomsoever the Son will reveal Him." *Matthew 11:27.* When one of the disciples made the request, "Show us the Father," Jesus answered, "Have I been so long time with you, and yet hast thou not known Me, Philip? He that hath seen Me hath seen the Father; and how sayest thou then, Show us the Father?" *John 14:8-9.*

In describing His earthly mission, Jesus said, The Lord "hath anointed Me to preach the gospel to the poor; He hath sent Me to heal the brokenhearted, to preach deliverance to the captives, and recovering of sight to the blind, to set at liberty them that are bruised." *Luke 4:18.* This was His work. He went about doing good and healing all that were oppressed by Satan. There were whole villages where there was not a moan of sickness in any house, for He had passed through them and healed all their sick. His work gave evidence of His divine anointing. Love, mercy, and compassion were revealed in every act of His life; His heart went out in tender sympathy to the children of men. He took man's nature, that He might reach man's wants. The poorest and humblest were not afraid to approach Him. Even little children were attracted to Him. They loved to climb upon His knees and gaze into the pensive face, benignant with love.

Always in Love

Jesus did not suppress one word of truth, but He uttered it always in love. He exercised the greatest tact and thoughtful, kind attention in His intercourse with the people. He was never rude, never needlessly spoke a severe word, never gave needless pain to a sensitive soul. He did not censure human weakness. He spoke the truth, but always in love. He denounced hypocrisy, unbelief, and iniquity; but tears were in His voice as He uttered His scathing rebukes. He wept over Jerusalem, the city He loved, which refused to receive Him, the way, the truth, and the life. They had rejected Him, the Saviour; but He regarded them with pitying tenderness. His life was one of self-denial and thoughtful care for others. Every soul was precious in His eyes. While He ever bore Himself with divine dignity, He bowed with the tenderest regard to every member of the family of God. In all men He saw fallen souls whom it was His mission to save.

Such is the character of Christ as revealed in His life. This is the character of God. It is from the Father's heart that the streams of divine compassion, manifest in Christ, flow out to the children of men. Jesus, the tender, pitying Saviour, was God "manifest in the flesh" (*1 Timothy 3:16*).

Behold Him

It was to redeem us that Jesus lived and suffered and died. He became "a Man of Sorrows," that we might be made partakers of everlasting joy. God permitted His beloved Son, full of grace and truth, to come from a world of indescribable glory, to a world marred and blighted with sin, darkened with the shadow of death and the curse. He permitted Him to leave the bosom of His love, the adoration of the angels, to suffer shame, insult, humiliation, hatred, and death. "The chastisement of our peace was upon Him; and with His stripes we are healed." *Isaiah 53:5*. Behold Him in the wilderness, in Gethsemane, upon the cross! The spotless Son of God took upon Himself the burden of sin. He who had been one with God, felt in His soul the awful separation that sin makes between God and man. This wrung from His lips the anguished cry, "My God, My God, why hast Thou forsaken Me?" *Matthew 27:46*. It was the burden of sin, the sense of its terrible enormity, of its separation of the soul from God—it was this that broke the heart of the Son of God.

But this great sacrifice was not made in order to create in the Father's heart a love for man, not to make Him willing to save. No, no! "God so loved the world, that He gave His only begotten Son." *John 3:16*. The Father loves us, not because of the great propitiation, but He provided the propitiation because He loves us. Christ was the medium through which He could pour out His infinite love upon a fallen world. "God was in Christ, reconciling the world unto Himself." *2 Corinthians 5:19*. God suffered with His Son. In the agony of Gethsemane, the death of Calvary, the heart of Infinite Love paid the price of our redemption.

Jesus said, "Therefore doth My Father love Me, because I lay down My life, that I might take it again." *John 10:17*. That is, "My Father has so loved you that He even loves Me more for giving My life to redeem you. In becoming your Substitute and Surety, by surrendering My life, by taking your liabilities, your transgressions, I am endeared to My Father; for, by My sacrifice, God can be just and yet the Justifier of him who believeth in Jesus."

Only Jesus Could Do It

None but the Son of God could accomplish our redemption; for only He who was in the bosom of the Father could declare Him. Only He who knew the height and depth of the love of God could make it manifest. Nothing less than the infinite sacrifice made by Christ, in behalf of fallen man could express the Father's love to lost humanity.

"God so loved the world, that He gave His only begotten Son." He gave Him not only to live among men, to bear their sins, and die their sacrifice. He gave Him to the fallen race. Christ was to identify Himself with the interests and needs of humanity. He who was one with God has linked Himself with the children of men by ties that are never to be broken. Jesus is "not ashamed to call them brethren" (*Hebrews 2:11*); He is our Sacrifice, our Advocate, our Brother, bearing our human form before the Father's throne, and through eternal ages one with the race He has redeemed—the Son of man. And all this that man might be uplifted from the ruin and degradation of sin that he might reflect the love of God and share the joy of holiness.

The price paid for our redemption, the infinite sacrifice of our heavenly Father, in giving His Son to die for us, should give us exalted conceptions of what we may become through Christ. As the inspired apostle John beheld the height, the depth, the breadth of the Father's love toward the perishing race, he was filled with adoration and reverence; and, failing to find suitable language in which to express the greatness and tenderness of this love, he called upon the world to behold it. "Behold, what manner of love the Father hath bestowed upon us, that we should be called the sons of God." *1 John 3:1*. What a value this places upon man! Through transgression the sons of man become subjects of Satan. Through faith in the atoning sacrifice of Christ the sons of Adam may become the sons of God. By assuming human nature, Christ elevates humanity. Fallen men are placed where, through connection with Christ, they may indeed become worthy of the name "sons of God."

A Love Beyond Measure

Such love is without a parallel. Children of the heavenly King! Precious promise! Theme for the most profound meditation! The matchless love of God for a world that did not love Him! The thought has a subduing power upon the soul and brings the mind into captivity to the will of God. The more we study the divine character in the light of the cross, the more we see mercy, tenderness, and forgiveness blended with equity and justice and the more clearly we discern innumerable evidences of a love that is infinite and a tender pity surpassing a mother's yearning sympathy for her wayward child.

For God so loved the world,
That He gave His only begotten Son,
That whosoever believeth in Him
Should not perish,
But have everlasting life.
— John 3:16

In this was manfested
The love of God toward us,
Because that God sent
His only begotten Son into the world,
That we might live through Him.
— 1 John 4:9

He that spared not His own Son,
But delivered Him up for us all;
How shall He not, with Him
Also freely give us all things?
— Romans 8:32

Behold, what manner of love
the Father hath bestowed upon us,
That we should be called
the Sons of God!
— 1 John 3:1

CHAPTER TWO

The Pathway Home

Andy had never had much in life, but he did have his two children and the little cabin in which they lived. Several years before, his wife had left the family one day, and later he learned that she had remarried, and then in an accident had been killed.

How Andy did love those children! And how he cared for them! They worked together on their little mountain farm, when the children were not at the little one-room schoolhouse down the road.

But then one day it happened.

Andy was out in the fields working when the fire started. But that morning both girls were in the house!

As soon as he saw the smoke he ran. His precious Suzy and Cindy! He prayed as he raced across the field and through a wooded area, for he had already learned by experience that God could answer prayer.

When he arrived, the little cabin was in flames. Smashing the door down with his powerful shoulder, he rushed in and found a blazing beam blocking a second door. Hurling it aside with his bare hands, he entered and found his little girls on the floor. Trying to put out the fire, they had both been overcome by the smoke. Reaching down with his strong arms, he picked them up and hurried from the blazing cabin.

Just as he set foot on the outside porch, the burning

rafters collapsed behind him into the building. Even yet, sparks and smoke and flame seemed everywhere, but somehow he struggled out into the yard. They were safe. Hearing about it, the local magistrate said that Andy's children must be taken from him and given to people who would give them a better home. This put the whole town in an uproar; and, on the day of the custody trial, the courtroom was packed.

First, the county attorney stood and told why he thought the children should be taken from Andy. The people respected him because he had lots of learning.

But then Andy got up. Too poor to afford a lawyer, he spoke for himself. With strong tears he told of his love and care for his little ones down through the years. No matter how bad the troubles got, he had given them his whole life—his all.

As he closed, he raised his hands and pled that the children might be restored to him. Reddened ugly scars disfigured both hands; for, in rescuing his beloved, the two hands had been severely burned.

At this, total silence came over the entire room and the judge tried to speak, but had a hard time getting the words out. Then he said this:

"Andy was willing to give his life for his children and he will carry the scars of his sacrifice in his hands for the remainder of his life. There is no one in this county better qualified to have them. This court rules that the children shall be given to Andy."

The whole building erupted in a burst of cheers, for Andy—who loved his own more than the whole world and had proved himself willing to die to save them—was now to receive his own back again.

Friend—just now—God wants to receive you back again also. On Calvary, Christ paid the price.

In the next few pages, you will learn why only He can give you the help you need to come back. He is the best Friend you will ever have.

Man was originally endowed with noble powers and a well-balanced mind. He was perfect in his being, and in harmony with God. His thoughts were pure, his aims holy. But through disobedience, his powers were perverted, and selfishness took the place of love. His nature became so weakened through transgression that it was impossible for him, in his own strength, to resist the power of evil. He was made captive by Satan, and would have remained so forever had not God specially interposed. It was the tempter's purpose to thwart the divine plan in man's creation and fill the earth with woe and desolation. And he would point to all this evil as the result of God's work in creating man.

In his sinless state, man held joyful communion with Him "in whom are hid all the treasures of wisdom and knowledge" (*Colossians 2:3*). But after his sin, he could no longer find joy in holiness, and he sought to hide from the presence of God. Such is still the condition of the unrenewed heart. It is not in harmony with God, and finds no joy in communion with Him. The sinner could not be happy in God's presence; he would shrink from the companionship of holy beings. Could he be permitted to enter heaven, it would have no joy for him. The spirit of unselfish love that reigns there—every heart responding to the heart of Infinite Love—would touch no answering chord in his soul. His thoughts, his interests, his motives, would be alien to those that actuate the sinless dwellers there. He would be a discordant note in the melody of heaven. Heaven would be to him a place of torture; he would long to be hidden from Him who is its light and the center of its joy. It is no arbitrary decree on the part of God that excludes the wicked from heaven; they are shut out by their own unfitness for its companionship. The glory of God would be to them a consuming fire. They would welcome destruction, that they might be hidden from the face of Him who died to redeem them.

It is impossible for us, of ourselves, to escape from the pit of sin in which we are sunken. Our hearts are evil, and we cannot change them. "Who can bring a clean thing out of an unclean? not one." *Job 14:4*. "The carnal mind is enmity against God: for it is not subject to the law of God, neither indeed can be." *Romans 8:7*. Education, culture, the exercise of the will, human effort, all have their proper sphere, but here they are powerless. They may produce an outward correctness of behavior, but they cannot change the heart; they cannot purify the springs of life. There must be a power working from within, a new life from above, before men can be changed from sin to holiness. That power is Christ. His grace alone can quicken the lifeless faculties of the soul and attract it to God, to holiness.

Only by a New Birth

The Saviour said, "Except a man be born from above," unless he shall receive a new heart, new desires, purposes, and motives, leading to a new life, "he cannot see the kingdom of God" (*John 3:3, margin*). The idea that it is necessary only to develop the good that exists in man, by nature, is a fatal deception. "The natural man receiveth not the things of the Spirit of God: for they are foolishness unto him: neither can he know them, because they are spiritually discerned."*1 Corinthians 2:14*. "Marvel not that I said unto thee, Ye must be born again." *John 3:7*. Of Christ it is written, "In Him was life; and the life was the light of men" . . there is no other "name under heaven given among men, whereby we must be saved" (*John 1:4; Acts 4:12*).

It is not enough to perceive the loving-kindness of God, to see the benevolence, the fatherly tenderness, of His character. It is not enough to discern the wisdom and justice of His law, to see that it is founded upon the eternal principle of love. Paul, the apostle, saw all this when he exclaimed, "I consent unto the law that it is good . . The law is holy, and the commandment holy, and just, and good." But he added, in the bitterness of his soul anguish and despair, "I am carnal, sold under sin" (*Romans 7:16, 12, 14*). He longed for the purity, the righteousness, to which in himself he was powerless to attain, and cried out, "O wretched man that I am! who shall deliver me from this body of death?" *Romans 7:24*. Such is the cry that has gone up from burdened hearts in all lands and in all ages. To all, there is but one answer, "Behold the Lamb of God, which taketh away the sin of the world." *John 1:29.*

The Ladder to Heaven

Many are the figures by which the Spirit of God has sought to illustrate this truth and make it plain to souls that long to be freed from the burden of guilt. When, after his sin in deceiving Esau, Jacob fled from his father's home, he was weighed down with a sense of guilt. Lonely and outcast as he was, separated from all that had made life dear, the one thought that above all others pressed upon his soul was the fear that his sin had cut him off from God, that he was forsaken of Heaven. In sadness he lay down to rest on the bare earth, around him only the lonely hills, and above, the heavens bright with stars. As he slept, a strange light broke upon his vision; and lo, from the plain on which he lay, vast shadowy stairs seemed to lead upward to the very gates of heaven, and upon them angels of God were passing up and down while, from the glory above, the divine voice was heard in a message of comfort and hope. Thus was made known to Jacob that which met the need and longing of his soul—a Saviour. With joy and gratitude he saw revealed a way by which he, a sinner, could be restored to communion with God. The mystic ladder of his dream represented Jesus, the only medium of communication between God and man.

This is the same figure to which Christ referred in His conversation with Nathanael, when He said, "Ye shall see heaven open, and the angels of God ascending and descending upon the Son of man." *John 1:51.* In the apostasy, man alienated himself from God; earth was cut off from heaven. Across the gulf that lay between, there could be no communion. But through Christ, earth is again linked with heaven. With His own merits, Christ has bridged the gulf which sin had made, so that the ministering angels can hold communion with man. Christ connects fallen man in his weakness and helplessness with the Source of infinite power.

Christ is the Only Way

But in vain are men's dreams of progress, in vain all efforts for the uplifting of humanity, if they neglect the one

Source of hope and help for the fallen race. "Every good gift and every perfect gift" (*James 1:17*) is from God. There is no true excellence of character apart from Him. And the only way to God is Christ. He says, "I am the way, the truth, and the life: no man cometh unto the Father, but by Me." *John 14:6.*

The heart of God yearns over His earthly children with a love stronger than death. In giving up His Son, He has poured out to us all heaven in one gift. The Saviour's life and death and intercession, the ministry of angels, the pleading of the Spirit, the Father working above and through all, the unceasing interest of heavenly beings,—all are enlisted in behalf of man's redemption.

Oh, let us contemplate the amazing sacrifice that has been made for us! Let us try to appreciate the labor and energy that Heaven is expending to reclaim the lost, and bring them back to the Father's house. Motives stronger, and agencies more powerful, could never be brought into operation; the exceeding rewards for rightdoing, the enjoyment of heaven, the society of the angels, the communion and love of God and His Son, the elevation and extension of all our powers throughout eternal ages—are these not mighty incentives and encouragements to urge us to give the heart's loving service to our Creator and Redeemer?

And, on the other hand, the judgments of God pronounced against sin, the inevitable retribution, the degradation of our character, and the final destruction are presented in God's Word to warn us against the service of Satan.

Shall we not regard the mercy of God? What more could He do? Let us place ourselves in right relation to Him who has loved us with amazing love. Let us avail ourselves of the means provided for us that we may be transformed into His likeness and be restored to fellowship with the ministering angels, to harmony and communion with the Father and the Son.

The fear of the Lord prolongeth days.
— Proverbs 10:27

CHAPTER THREE

Coming in Repentance

As Father stepped out of the farmhouse one morning, he noticed that a strong wind was coming from the west. "It's blowing up a freshet from the west,"

He said, as he headed toward the barn to repair the plow. He was thankful that the harvest had been completed the day before and now was stored safely in the barn. If a rain came now, it could not hurt the wheat. And, no doubt, a rain was needed. Everything was dry.

Then he stopped in his tracks: There was something unusual about that wind! Yes, now he knew: It carried a telltale hint of smoke.

Quickly, Father ran back to the house. The girls were helping Mother clean up the breakfast dishes and his son Jim was pulling on his work boots.

"A prairie fire is coming!" Father cried. "We must work quickly!"

In spite of the urgency that now pressed like a weight upon each one, they all knelt together in that kitchen and prayed around the circle: each one pleading with God to save their farm.

"Jim, hitch up the team to the plow!" "Father, we can't," Jim cried. "The plow's broken!"

"I forgot. So we can't use it to plow a firebreak; we'll have to set a backfire! Helen, you and the girls begin hauling water out of the well. Fill every container. We'll need it if the sides of the buildings start smoking."

Out on the prairies, the grass stretches on for miles over the rolling land. Back in the old days, when a fire started somewhere, it could, depending on the dryness of the countryside and the velocity of the wind, travel for long distances.

By now, Father noticed that a strong wind was blowing as he and Jim began carefully setting backfires. They knew that upwind somewhere was a far bigger fire. And it was headed their way.

With the stiff wind, even backfires were not safe, and progress went slowly. When it came time for lunch, they ate hurriedly as they kept working.

Fortunately, they had an early warning of what was coming. By afternoon, the smell of smoke was becoming stronger, but the rolling plains hid the flames from their sight. All they could do was watch and pray and work.

Sunset came early that evening. The air was filled with heavy smoke, and soon—in the deepening darkness, the advancing flames could be seen. Closer and closer they came. Would the firebreak hold? Was it wide enough? Would it divert the blaze?

With their eyes riveted to the west, the family watched as the flames drew nearer and reached the burned-over area where the backfire had been set. The smoke in their nostrils and the heat on their faces was almost impossible to bear.

And then it happened! As they watched, the wall of advancing flame grew higher, threatening to engulf them—and then began to die down in the center—and move to the right and left! The firebreak held!

The fire cannot come—where the fire has already been!

The fire fell at Calvary, when Christ died. If you come to Him now, He can forgive you and enable you by His grace to obey His Written Word.

In this chapter you will learn how to come:

How shall a man be just with God? How shall the sinner be made righteous? It is only through Christ that we can be brought into harmony with God, with holiness; but how are we to come to Christ? Many are asking the same question as did the multitude on the Day of Pentecost, when, convicted of sin, they cried out, "What shall we do?" The first word of Peter's answer was, "Repent." *Acts 2:37-38.* At another time, shortly after, he said, "Repent, . . and be converted, that your sins may be blotted out." *Acts 3:19.*

Repentance includes sorrow for sin and a turning away from it. We shall not renounce sin unless we see its sinfulness; until we turn away from it in heart, there will be no real change in the life.

There are many who fail to understand the true nature of repentance. Multitudes sorrow that they have sinned and even make an outward reformation because they fear that their wrongdoing will bring suffering upon themselves. But this is not repentance in the Bible sense. They lament the suffering rather than the sin. Such was the grief of Esau when he saw that the birthright was lost to him forever. Balaam, terrified by the angel standing in his pathway with drawn sword, acknowledged his guilt lest he should lose his life; but there was no genuine repentance for sin, no conversion of purpose, no abhorrence of evil. Judas Iscariot, after betraying his Lord, exclaimed, "I have sinned in that I have betrayed the innocent blood." *Matthew 27:4.*

Genuine Repentance

The confession was forced from his guilty soul by an awful sense of condemnation and a fearful looking for of judgment. The consequences that were to result to him filled him with terror, but there was no deep, heartbreaking grief in his soul, that he had betrayed the spotless Son of God and denied the Holy One of Israel. Pharaoh, when suffering under the judgments of God, acknowledged his sin in order to escape further punishment, but returned to his defiance of Heaven as soon as the plagues were stayed. These all lamented the results of sin, but did not sorrow for the sin itself.

But when the heart yields to the influence of the Spirit of God, the conscience will be quickened and the sinner will discern something of the depth and sacredness of God's holy law, the foundation of His government in heaven and on earth. The "Light, which lighteth every man that cometh into the world" (*John 1:9*) illumines the secret chambers of the soul, and the hidden things of darkness are made manifest. Conviction takes hold upon the mind and heart. The sinner has a sense of the righteousness of Jehovah and feels the terror of appearing, in his own guilt and uncleanness, before the Searcher of hearts. He sees the love of God, the beauty of holiness, the joy of purity; he longs to be cleansed and to be restored to communion with Heaven.

Sincere and Deep

The prayer of David, after his fall, illustrates the nature of true sorrow for sin. His repentance was sincere and deep. There was no effort to palliate his guilt; no desire to escape the judgment threatened inspired his prayer. David saw the enormity of his transgression; he saw the defilement of his soul; he loathed his sin. It was not for pardon only that he prayed, but for purity of heart. He longed for the joy of holiness—to be restored to harmony and communion with God. This was the language of his soul:

"Blessed is he whose transgression is forgiven, whose sin is covered. Blessed is the man unto whom the Lord imputeth not iniquity, and in whose spirit there is no guile." *Psalm 32:1-2*. "Have mercy upon me, O God, according to Thy lovingkindness: According unto the multitude of Thy tender mercies blot out my transgressions . . For I acknowledge my transgressions: and my sin is ever before me . . Purge me with hyssop, and I shall be clean: wash me, and I shall be whiter than snow . . Create in me a clean heart, O God; and renew a right spirit within me. Cast me not away from Thy presence; and take not Thy Holy Spirit from me. Restore unto me the joy of Thy salvation; and uphold me with Thy free spirit . . Deliver me from bloodguiltiness, O God, Thou God of my salvation: and my tongue shall sing aloud of Thy righteousness." *Psalm 51:1, 3, 7, 10-12, 14*.

A repentance such as this is beyond the reach of our own power to accomplish; it is obtained only from Christ, who ascended up on high and has given gifts unto men.

Do Not Wait - Come

Just here is a point on which many may err, and hence they fail of receiving the help that Christ desires to give them. They think that they cannot come to Christ unless they first repent, and that repentance prepares for the forgiveness of their sins. It is true that repentance does precede the forgiveness of sins; for it is only the broken and contrite heart that will feel the need of a Saviour. But must the sinner wait till he has repented before he can come to Jesus? Is repentance to be made an obstacle between the sinner and the Saviour?

The Bible does not teach that the sinner must repent before he can heed the invitation of Christ, "Come unto Me, all ye that labor and are heavy laden, and I will give you rest." *Matthew 11:28.* It is the virtue that goes forth from Christ, that leads to genuine repentance. Peter made the matter clear in his statement to the Israelites when he said, "Him hath God exalted with His right hand to be a Prince and a Saviour, for to give repentance to Israel, and forgiveness of sins." *Acts 5:31.* We can no more repent without the Spirit of Christ to awaken the conscience than we can be pardoned without Christ.

Christ is the source of every right impulse. He is the only one that can implant in the heart enmity against sin. Every desire for truth and purity, every conviction of our own sinfulness, is an evidence that His Spirit is moving upon our hearts.

Look and Live

Jesus has said, "I, if I be lifted up from the earth, will draw all men unto Me." *John 12:32.* Christ must be revealed to the sinner as the Saviour dying for the sins of the world; and as we behold the Lamb of God upon the cross of Calvary, the mystery of redemption begins to unfold to our minds and the goodness of God leads us to repentance. In dying for sinners, Christ manifested a love that is incomprehensible; and, as the sinner beholds this love, it softens the heart, impresses the mind, and inspires contrition in the soul.

It is true that men sometimes become ashamed of their sinful ways and give up some of their evil habits before they are conscious that they are being drawn to Christ. But whenever they make an effort to reform, from a sincere desire to do right, it is the power of Christ that is drawing them. An influence of which they are unconscious works upon the soul, the conscience is quickened, and the outward life is amended. And as Christ draws them to look upon His cross, to behold Him whom their sins have pierced, the commandment comes home to the conscience. The wickedness of their life, the deep-seated sin of the soul, is revealed to them. They begin to comprehend something of the righteousness of Christ, and exclaim, "What is sin, that it should require such a sacrifice for the redemption of its victim? Was all this love, all this suffering, all this humiliation demanded, that we might not perish, but have everlasting life?"

The sinner may resist this love, may refuse to be drawn to Christ; but, if he does not resist, he will be drawn to Jesus. A knowledge of the plan of salvation will lead him to the foot of the cross in repentance for his sins, which have caused the sufferings of God's dear Son.

The same divine mind that is working upon the things of nature is speaking to the hearts of men and creating an inexpressible craving for something they have not. The things of the world cannot satisfy their longing. The Spirit of God is pleading with them to seek for those things that alone can give peace and rest—the grace of Christ, the joy of holiness. Through influences seen and unseen, our Saviour is constantly at work to attract the minds of men from the unsatisfying pleasures of sin to the infinite blessings that may be theirs in Him. To all these souls who are vainly seeking to drink from the broken cisterns of this world, the divine message is addressed, "Let him that is athirst come. And whosoever will, let him take the water of life freely." *Revelation 22:17.*

Ask and Receive

You who in heart long for something better than this world can give recognize this longing as the voice of God to your soul. Ask Him to give you repentance, to reveal Christ to you in His infinite love, in His perfect purity. In the Saviour's life the principles of God's law—love to God and man—were perfectly exemplified. Benevolence, unselfish love, was the life of His soul. It is as we behold Him, as the light from our Saviour falls upon us, that we see the sinfulness of our own hearts.

We may have flattered ourselves, as did Nicodemus, that our life has been upright, that our moral character is correct, and think that we need not humble the heart before God, like the common sinner; but, when the light from Christ shines into our souls, we shall see how impure we are. We shall discern the selfishness of motive, the enmity against God, that has defiled every act of life. Then we shall know that our own righteousness is indeed as filthy rags and that the blood of Christ alone can cleanse us from the defilement of sin and renew our hearts in His own likeness.

We Need to See Him

One ray of the glory of God, one gleam of the purity of Christ, penetrating the soul, makes every spot of defilement painfully distinct and lays bare the deformity and defects of the human character. It makes apparent the unhallowed desires, the infidelity of the heart, the impurity of the lips. The sinner's acts of disloyalty, in making void the law of God, are exposed to his sight, and his spirit is stricken and afflicted under the searching influence of the Spirit of God. He loathes himself as he views the pure, spotless character of Christ.

When the prophet, Daniel, beheld the glory surrounding the heavenly messenger that was sent unto him, he was overwhelmed with a sense of his own weakness and imperfection. Describing the effect of the wonderful scene, he says, "There remained no strength in me: for my comeliness was turned in me into corruption, and I retained no strength." *Daniel 10:8*. The soul thus touched will hate its selfishness, abhor its self-love, and will seek, through Christ's righteousness, for the purity of heart that is in harmony with the law of God and the character of Christ.

Understanding God's Law

Paul says that as "touching the righteousness which is in the law"—as far as outward acts were concerned—he was "blameless" (*Philippians 3:6*); but, when the spiritual character of the law was discerned, he saw himself a sinner. Judged by the letter of the law as men apply it to the outward life, he had abstained from sin; but, when he looked into the depths of its holy precepts and saw himself as God saw him, he bowed in humiliation and confessed his guilt. He says, "I was alive without the law once: but when the commandment came, sin revived, and I died." *Romans 7:9*. When he saw the spiritual nature of the law, sin appeared in its true hideousness, and his self-esteem was gone.

God does not regard all sins as of equal magnitude; there are degrees of guilt in His estimation, as well as in that of man; but, however trifling this or that wrong act may seem in the eyes of men, no sin is small in the sight of God. Man's judgment is partial, imperfect; but God estimates all things as they really are. The drunkard is despised and is told that his sin will exclude him from heaven while pride, selfishness, and covetousness too often go unrebuked. But these are sins that are especially offensive to God; for they are contrary to the benevolence of His character, to that unselfish love which is the very atmosphere of the unfallen universe. He who falls into some of the grosser sins may feel a sense of his shame and poverty and his need of the grace of Christ; but pride feels no need, and so it closes the heart against Christ and the infinite blessings He came to give.

The poor publican who prayed, "God be merciful to me a sinner" (*Luke 18:13*), regarded himself as a very wicked man. Others looked upon him in the same light; but he felt his need; and, with his burden of guilt and shame he came before God, asking for His mercy. His heart was open for the Spirit of God to do its gracious work and set him free from the power of sin. The Pharisee's boastful, self-righteous prayer showed that his heart was closed against the influence of the Holy Spirit. Because of his distance from God, he had no sense of his own defilement, in contrast with the perfection of the divine holiness. He felt no need, and he received nothing.

Come Today

If you see your sinfulness, do not wait to make yourself better. How many there are who think they are not good enough to come to Christ. Do you expect to become better through your own efforts? "Can the Ethiopian change his skin, or the leopard his spots? then may ye also do good, that are accustomed to do evil." *Jeremiah 13:23*. There is help for us only in God. We must not wait for stronger persuasions, for better opportunities, or for holier tempers. We can do nothing of ourselves. We must come to Christ just as we are.

There Was No Other Way

But let none deceive themselves with the thought that God, in His great love and mercy, will yet save even the rejecters of His grace. The exceeding sinfulness of sin can be estimated only in the light of the cross. When men urge that God is too good to cast off the sinner, let them look to Calvary. It was because there was no other way in which man could be saved; because, without this sacrifice, it was impossible for the human race to escape from the defiling power of sin, and be restored to communion with holy beings,—impossible for them again to become partakers of spiritual life,—it was because of this that Christ took upon Himself the guilt of the disobedient and suffered in the sinner's stead. The love and suffering and death of the Son of God all testify to the terrible enormity of sin and declare that there is no escape from its power, no hope of the higher life, but through the submission of the soul to Christ.

The impenitent sometimes excuse themselves by saying of professed Christians, "I am as good as they are. They are no more self-denying, sober, or circumspect in their conduct than I am. They love pleasure and self-indulgence as well as I do." Thus they make the faults of others an excuse for their own neglect of duty. But the sins and defects of others do not excuse anyone, for the Lord has not given us an erring human pattern. The spotless Son of God has been given as our example, and those who complain of the wrong course of professed Christians are the ones who should show better lives and nobler examples. If they have so high a conception of what a Christian should be, is not their own sin so much the greater? They know what is right, and yet refuse to do it.

A Terrible Danger in Delay

Beware of procrastination. Do not put off the work of forsaking your sins and seeking purity of heart through Jesus. Here is where thousands upon thousands have erred to their eternal loss. I will not here dwell upon the shortness and uncertainty of life; but there is a terrible danger—a danger not sufficiently understood—in delaying to yield to the pleading voice of God's Holy Spirit, in choosing to live in sin; for such this delay really is. Sin, however small it may be esteemed, can be indulged in only at the peril of infinite loss. What we do not overcome will overcome us and work out our destruction.

Adam and Eve persuaded themselves that, in so small a matter as eating of the forbidden fruit, there could not result such terrible consequences as God had declared. But this small matter was the transgression of God's immutable and holy law, and it separated man from God and opened the floodgates of death and untold woe upon our world. Age after age, there has gone up from our earth a continual cry of mourning, and the whole creation groaneth and travaileth together in pain as a consequence of man's disobedience. Heaven itself has felt the effects of his rebellion against God. Calvary stands as a memorial of the amazing sacrifice required to atone for the transgression of the divine law. Let us not regard sin as a trivial thing.

Every act of transgression, every neglect or rejection of the grace of Christ is reacting upon yourself; it is hardening the heart, depraving the will, benumbing the understanding, and not only making you less inclined to yield, but less capable of yielding to the tender pleading of God's Holy Spirit.

Not Easier Later On

Many are quieting a troubled conscience with the thought that they can change a course of evil when they choose; that they can trifle with the invitations of mercy, and yet be again and again impressed. They think that after doing despite to the Spirit of grace, after casting their influence on the side of Satan, in a moment of terrible extremity they can change their course. But this is not so easily done. The experience, the education, of a lifetime has so thoroughly molded the character that few then desire to receive the image of Jesus.

Even one wrong trait of character, one sinful desire, persistently cherished, will eventually neutralize all the power of the gospel. Every sinful indulgence strengthens the soul's aversion to God. The man who manifests an infidel hardihood or a stolid indifference to divine truth is but reaping the harvest of that which he has himself sown. In all the Bible there is not a more fearful warning against trifling with evil than the words of the wise man that the sinner "shall be holden with the cords of his sins." *Proverbs 5:22.*

Ready and Waiting

Christ is ready to set us free from sin, but He does not force the will; and if, by persistent transgression, the will itself is wholly bent on evil and we do not desire to be set free, if we will not accept His grace, what more can He do? We have destroyed ourselves by our determined rejection of His love. "Behold, now is the accepted time; behold, now is the day of salvation." *2 Corinthians 6:2.* "Today if ye will hear His voice, harden not your hearts." *Hebrews 3:7-8.*

"Man looketh on the outward appearance, but the Lord looketh on the heart" (*1 Samuel 16:7*)—the human heart, with its conflicting emotions of joy and sorrow; the wandering, wayward heart, which is the abode of so much impurity and deceit. He knows its motives, its very intents and purposes. Go to Him with your soul all stained as it is. Like the psalmist, throw its chambers open to the all-seeing eye, exclaiming, "Search me, O God, and know my heart: try me, and know my thoughts: and see if there be any wicked way in me, and lead me in the way everlasting." *Psalm 139:23-*

24.

Many accept an intellectual religion, a form of godliness, when the heart is not cleansed. Let it be your prayer, "Create in me a clean heart, O God; and renew a right spirit within me." *Psalm 51:10.* Deal truly with your own soul. Be as earnest, as persistent, as you would be if your mortal life were at stake. This is a matter to be settled between God and your own soul, settled for eternity. A supposed hope, and nothing more, will prove your ruin.

Study God's Word prayerfully. That Word presents before you, in the law of God and the life of Christ, the great principles of holiness, without which "no man shall see the Lord." *Hebrews 12:14.* It convinces of sin; it plainly reveals the way of salvation. Give heed to it as the voice of God speaking to your soul.

He Came to Save You

As you see the enormity of sin, as you see yourself as you really are, do not give up to despair. It was sinners that Christ came to save. We have not to reconcile God to us, but—O wondrous love!—God in Christ is "reconciling the world unto Himself." *2 Corinthians 5:19.* He is wooing by His tender love the hearts of His erring children. No earthly parent could be as patient with the faults and mistakes of his children as is God with those He seeks to save. No one could plead more tenderly with the transgressor. No human lips ever poured out more tender entreaties to the wanderer than does He. All His promises, His warnings, are but the breathing of unutterable love.

When Satan comes to tell you that you are a great sinner, look up to your Redeemer and talk of His merits. That which will help you is to look to His light. Acknowledge your sin, but tell the enemy that "Christ Jesus came into the world to save sinners" and that you may be saved by His matchless love. *1 Timothy 1:15.* Jesus asked Simon a question in regard to two debtors. One owed his lord a small sum and the other owed him a very large sum; but he forgave them both, and Christ asked Simon which debtor would love his lord most. Simon answered, "He to whom he forgave most." *Luke 7:43.* We have been great sinners, but Christ died that we might be forgiven. The merits of His sacrifice are sufficient to present to the Father in our behalf. Those to whom He has forgiven most will love Him most, and will stand nearest to His throne to praise Him for His great love and infinite sacrifice. It is when we most fully comprehend the love of God that we best realize the sinfulness of sin. When we see the length of the chain that was let down for us, when we understand something of the infinite sacrifice that Christ has made in our behalf, the heart is melted with tenderness and contrition.

How excellent is Thy lovingkindness,
O God!
Therefore the children of men
Put their trust
Under the shadow of Thy wings.
— Psalm 36:7

Beloved, if God so loved us,
We ought also to love one another.
— 1 John 4:11

And she shall bring forth a son,
And thou shalt call His name Jesus:
For He shall save His people from their sins.
— Matthew 1:21

Whosoever committeth sin
Transgresseth also the law:
For sin is the transgression of the law.
— 1 John 3:4

In everything
By prayer and supplication
With thanksgiving,
Let your requests
Be made known unto God.
— Philippians 4:6

BIBLE PROMISES YOU CAN USE

The Lord, He it is that doth go before thee; He will be with thee: He will not fail thee, neither forsake thee.

– *Deuteronomy 31:8* .

The Lord God is a sun and shield: the Lord will give grace and glory; no good thing will He withhold from them that walk uprightly. – *Psalm 84:11.*

The mountains shall depart, and the hills be removed; but My kindness shall not depart from thee, neither shall the covenant of My peace be removed, saith the Lord that hath mercy on thee.

– *Isaiah 54:10.*

Surely I know that it shall be well with them that fear God, which fear before Him. – *Ecclesiastes 8:12.*

Verily there is a reward for the righteous. – *Psalm 58:11.*

Godliness is profitable unto all things, having promise of the life that now is, and of that which is to come.

– *1 Timothy 4:8.*

The Lord is my Shepherd, I shall not want . . Thou preparest a table before me in the presence of mine enemies; Thou anointest my head with oil, my cup runneth over.

– *Psalm 23:1, 5.*

Seek ye first the kingdom of God and His righteousness, and all these things shall be added unto you.

– *Matthew 6:33.*

My God shall supply all your need according to His riches in glory by Christ Jesus. – *Philippians 4:19.*

Trust in the Lord and do good; so shalt thou dwell in the land, and verily thou shalt be fed. – *Psalm 37:3.*

Behold the fowls of the air, . . yet your heavenly Father feedeth them. Are ye not much better than they?

– *Matthew 6:26.*

Ye shall walk in all the ways which the Lord your God hath commanded you, that ye may live, and that it may be well with you, and that ye may prolong your days in the land which ye shall possess. – *Deuteronomy 5:33.*

With long life will I satisfy him, and show him My salvation.

– *Psalm 91:16.*

The name of the Lord is a strong tower; the righteous runneth into it, and is safe. – *Proverbs 18:10.*

CHAPTER FOUR

Giving Him Your Sins

Repentance is the next step in coming. What is genuine repentance? Let me explain it:

If there is no repentance, there can be no pardon.

About fifty-five years ago, John Hansen was sentenced to death.

But the murderer's brother besought the governor of the State for a pardon for him. Because Howard Hansen was very influential, and because the State was indebted to him for former services, the pardon was granted.

With the pardon in his coat pocket, Howard went to the state penitentiary. When the two were together, he asked, "John, what would you do if you received a pardon?"

"The first thing I would do," John answered, "is to track down the judge who sentenced me, and murder him; and the next thing I would do is find the chief witness and kill him."

The brother arose and left the prison—with the pardon still in his pocket.

But when it is a genuine repentance, the God of heaven can, and will, give an even greater pardon!

Let me explain:

By the time Robert Gallagher was a teenager, he knew

he needed help, but he didn't know where to get it. Then one night, he stepped inside a church and heard a country preacher talk about "The Gates of Heaven."

He was startled; for he knew that, if the gates of heaven were opened that night, he could not enter—because of the kind of life he was living.

The next night the topic was the Bible verse, "What shall I do then with Jesus who is called the Christ?" (Matthew 27:22). Robert went home utterly wretched. Unable to sleep, he finally arose and went out and gazed up at the stars. It was a clear night, and he knew that somewhere up there was the home he wanted. Oh, how he wanted to make his peace with God! But his sins seemed to rise up like a mountain before him.

The next day he had to plow. His misery deepened with every furrow, until finally he drove out to the end of a long row and dropped the plow down by the side of Barney, the old white mule.

Before him was a weathered rail fence, and he got down on his knees in the fence corner and told God his sins. He cried for forgiveness and help. He pled for pardon and peace.

He asked for strength to begin a new, clean life. He could not leave until it was taken care of! His repentance was deep, and the sense of forgiveness that God gave him there was full and deep.

That evening there was another meeting, and again he went. What they talked about that night, he doesn't recall; but he walked down the aisle and told everyone he had accepted Christ as his Saviour—and that henceforth he was giving his life to Him.

But he does remember the hymn they sang. He will never forget it:

"Out of my bondage, sorrow, and night;
Jesus, I come! Jesus, I come!
Into Thy freedom, gladness, and light;
Jesus, I come to Thee!"

"He that covereth his sins shall not prosper: but whoso confesseth and forsaketh them shall have mercy." *Proverbs 28:13.*

The conditions of obtaining the mercy of God are simple and just and reasonable. The Lord does not require us to do some grievous thing in order that we may have the forgiveness of sin. We need not make long and wearisome pilgrimages or perform painful penances to commend our souls to the God of heaven or to expiate our transgression; but he that confesseth and forsaketh his sin shall have mercy.

The apostle says, "Confess your faults one to another, and pray one for another, that ye may be healed." *James 5:16.* Confess your sins to God, who only can forgive them, and your faults to one another. If you have given offense to your friend or neighbor, you are to acknowledge your wrong; and it is his duty freely to forgive you. Then you are to seek the forgiveness of God, because the brother you have wounded is the property of God; and, in injuring him, you sinned against his Creator and Redeemer. The case is brought before the only true Mediator, our great High Priest, who "was in all points tempted like as we are, yet without sin," and who is "touched with the feeling of our infirmities" (*Hebrews 4:15*) and is able to cleanse from every stain of iniquity.

Those who have not humbled their souls before God in acknowledging their guilt have not yet fulfilled the first condition of acceptance. If we have not experienced that repentance which is not to be repented of, and have not with true humiliation of soul and brokenness of spirit confessed our sins, abhorring our iniquity, we have never truly sought for the forgiveness of sin; and, if we have never sought, we have never found the peace of God. The only reason why we do not have remission of sins that are past is that we are not willing to humble our hearts and comply with the conditions of the Word of truth. Explicit instruction is given concerning this matter. Confession of sin, whether public or private, should be heartfelt and freely expressed. It is not to be urged from the sinner. It is not to be made in a flippant and careless way or forced from those who have no realization of the abhorrent character of sin. The confession that is the outpouring of the inmost soul finds its way to the God of infinite pity. The psalmist says, "The Lord is nigh unto them that are of a broken heart; and saveth such as be of a contrite spirit." *Psalm 34:18.*

True Confession

True confession is always of a specific character, and acknowledges particular sins. They may be of such a nature as to be brought before God only; they may be wrongs that should be confessed to individuals who have suffered injury through them; or they may be of a public character, and should then be as publicly confessed. But all confession should be definite and to the point, acknowledging the very sins of which you are guilty.

In the days of Samuel the Israelites wandered from God. They were suffering the consequences of sin; for they had lost their faith in God, lost their discernment of His power and wisdom to rule the nation, lost their confidence in His ability to defend and vindicate His cause. They turned from the great Ruler of the universe and desired to be governed as were the nations around them. Before they found peace they made this definite confession: "We have added unto all our sins this evil, to ask us a king." *1 Samuel 12:19.* The very sin of which they were convicted had to be confessed. Their ingratitude oppressed their souls and severed them from God.

Confession will not be acceptable to God without sincere repentance and reformation. There must be decided changes in the life; everything offensive to God must be put away. This will be the result of genuine sorrow for sin. The work that we have to do on our part is plainly set before us: "Wash you, make you clean; put away the evil of your doings from before Mine eyes; cease to do evil; learn to do well; seek judgment, relieve the oppressed, judge the fatherless, plead for the widow." *Isaiah 1:16-17.* "If the wicked restore the pledge, give again that he had robbed, walk in the statutes of life, without committing iniquity; he shall surely live, he shall not die." *Ezekiel 33:15.* Paul says, speaking of the work of repentance: "Ye sorrowed after a godly sort, what carefulness it wrought in you, yea, what clearing of yourselves, yea, what indignation, yea, what fear, yea, what vehement desire, yea, what zeal, yea, what revenge! In all things ye have approved yourselves to be clear in this matter." 2 *Corinthians 7:11.*

An Acknowledgment, Not an Excuse

When sin has deadened the moral perceptions, the wrongdoer does not discern the defects of his character nor realize the enormity of the evil he has committed; and, unless he yields to the convicting power of the Holy Spirit, he remains in partial blindness to his sin. His confessions are not sincere and in earnest. To every acknowledgment of his guilt he adds an apology in excuse of his course, declaring that if it had not been for certain circumstances he would not have done this or that for which he is reproved.

After Adam and Eve had eaten of the forbidden fruit, they were filled with a sense of shame and terror. At first their only thought was how to excuse their sin and escape the dreaded sentence of death. When the Lord inquired concerning their sin, Adam replied, laying the guilt partly upon God and partly upon his companion: "The woman whom Thou gavest to be with me, she gave me of the tree, and I did eat." The woman put the blame upon the serpent, saying, "The serpent beguiled me, and I did eat." *Genesis 3:12-13.* Why did You make the serpent? Why did You suffer him to come into Eden? These were the questions implied in her excuse for her sin, thus charging God with the responsibility of their fall. The spirit of self-justification originated in the father of lies and has been exhibited by all the sons and daughters of Adam. Confessions of this order are not inspired by the divine Spirit and will not be acceptable to God. True repentance will lead a man to bear his guilt himself and acknowledge it without deception or hypocrisy. Like the poor publican, not lifting up so much as his eyes unto heaven, he will cry, "God be merciful to me a sinner" and those who do acknowledge their guilt will be justified; for Jesus will plead

His blood in behalf of the repentant soul.

No Self-Justification

The examples in God's Word of genuine repentance and humiliation reveal a spirit of confession in which there is no excuse for sin or attempt at self-justification. Paul did not seek to shield himself; he paints his sin in its darkest hue, not attempting to lessen his guilt. He says, "Many of the saints did I shut up in prison, having received authority from the chief priests; and when they were put to death, I gave my voice against them. And I punished them oft in every synagogue, and compelled them to blaspheme; and being exceedingly mad against them, I persecuted them even unto strange cities." *Acts 26:10-11*. He does not hesitate to declare that "Christ Jesus came into the world to save sinners; of whom I am chief" (*1 Timothy 1:15*).

The humble and broken heart, subdued by genuine repentance, will appreciate something of the love of God and the cost of Calvary; and, as a son confesses to a loving father, so will the truly penitent bring all his sins before God. And it is written, "If we confess our sins, He is faithful and just to forgive us our sins, and to cleanse us from all unrighteousness." *1 John 1:9*.

And it shall come to pass,
When all these things are come upon thee,
The blessing and the curse,
Which I set before thee,
And thou shalt call them to mind . .
And shalt return unto the Lord thy God,
And shalt obey His voice
According to all that I command thee, . .
That the Lord thy God will turn thy captivity,
And have compassion upon thee, . .
If thou shalt hearken
Unto the voice of the Lord thy God,
To keep His commandments . .
And if thou turn unto the Lord thy God
With all thine heart, and with all thy soul.
— Deuteronomy 30:1-3, 10

CHAPTER FIVE

Giving Him Your Life

A wealthy Englishman found a rare violin; and, at great expense, he added it to his collection. One day, Fritz Kreisler, the famous violinist, visited at his home and, seeing it, recognized its value.

He asked if he could purchase it from the businessman, for it was obvious that Mr. Kreisler could draw from it that which the Englishman never could. But, collector that he was, the man felt he dare not part from it, for the violin looked so nice lying on his shelf. Then Mr. Kreisler asked if he could play the rare violin but once. The Englishman consented,—and stood entranced as Fritz Kreisler, one of the greatest violinists in the world, played it. Forgetting himself, Kreisler poured his heart into the music.

Finally the musical harmonies ceased. Again the violin was silent. The Englishman was speechless. He watched as Kreisler tenderly returned the valuable instrument to its antique box, with all the gentleness of a mother putting her baby to bed.

"Take the violin," the Englishman burst out; "it is yours! I have no right to keep it. It ought to belong to the man who can bring such music out of it as you can."

Just now, as you think back upon your past life, and then upon your present circumstances, everything

may seem to be full of tangled threads and of little value.

But dedicated to God, your life can take on a new meaning,—and a worth that you have never experienced before. Placed in His hands, you gain immensely in value and usefulness.

Your life ought to belong to the only One who can impart to it nobility of character and bring from it the sweet beauty of a deep Christian experience.

This is the consecration—the dedication—of your life to God that you want. Give your violin—your mind and body and purposes—to your Creator, henceforth to let Him use it for His glory.

For decades, David Livingstone traveled thousands of miles through the heart of Africa preaching Christ and exploring the land, so that Christian missionaries could enter the country.

Then, after thirty years of such intense difficulty, Henry Stanley finally found him. Livingstone had been lost to the world for over two years. Stanley asked him to come back with him to England, but Livingstone refused.

Two days later, Livingstone wrote in his diary, "March 19th, my birthday. My Jesus, my King, my Life, my All; I again dedicate my whole self to Thee. Accept me, and grant, O gracious Father, that when the year is gone I may finish my work. In Jesus' name, I ask it, Amen." A year later, his servants found him dead on his knees, where he had been praying.

What is a dedicated life? It is to give all that you have to God, and let Him use you to do the work that, in His great plan, He has assigned you on this earth.

The continued peace of heart that an individual can have who is living and walking with God,—can only be known by the one who has experienced it.

And this is your heavenly Father's plan for you. Come, just now, and make His plan your own.

God's promise is, "Ye shall seek Me, and find Me, when ye shall search for Me with all your heart." *Jeremiah 29:13.*

The whole heart must be yielded to God or the change can never be wrought in us by which we are to be restored to His likeness. By nature we are alienated from God. The Holy Spirit describes our condition in such words as these: "Dead in trespasses and sins" (*Ephesians 2:1*), "the whole head is sick, and the whole heart faint . . no soundness in it" (*Isaiah 1:5-6*). We are held fast in the snare of Satan, "taken captive by him at his will" (*2 Timothy 2:26*). God desires to heal us, to set us free. But since this requires an entire transformation, a renewing of our whole nature, we must yield ourselves wholly to Him.

The warfare against self is the greatest battle that was ever fought. The yielding of self, surrendering all to the will of God, requires a struggle; but the soul must submit to God before it can be renewed in holiness.

The government of God is not, as Satan would make it appear, founded upon a blind submission, an unreasoning control. It appeals to the intellect and the conscience. "Come now, and let us reason together" (*Isaiah 1:18*) is the Creator's invitation to the beings He has made. God does not force the will of His creatures. He cannot accept a homage that is not willingly and intelligently given. A mere forced submission would prevent all real development of mind or character; it would make man a mere automaton. Such is not the purpose of the Creator. He desires that man, the crowning work of His creative power, shall reach the highest possible development. He sets before us the height of blessing to which He desires to bring us through His grace. He invites us to give ourselves to Him, that He may work His will in us. It remains for us to choose whether we will be set free from the bondage of sin, to share the glorious liberty of the sons of God.

In giving ourselves to God, we must necessarily give up all that would separate us from Him. Hence the Saviour says, "Whosoever he be of you that forsaketh not all that he hath, he cannot be My disciple." *Luke 14:33.* Whatever shall draw away the heart from God must be given up. Mammon is the idol of many. The love of money, the desire for wealth, is the golden chain that binds them to Satan. Reputation and worldly honor are worshiped by another class. The life of selfish ease and freedom from responsibility is the idol of others. But these slavish bands must be broken. We cannot be half the Lord's and half the world's. We are not God's children unless we are such entirely.

More than a Mere Profession

There are those who profess to serve God while they rely upon their own efforts to obey His law, to form a right character, and secure salvation. Their hearts are not moved by any deep sense of the love of Christ, but they seek to perform the duties of the Christian life as that which God requires of them in order to gain heaven. Such religion is worth nothing. When Christ dwells in the heart, the soul will be so filled with His love, with the joy of communion with Him, that it will cleave to Him; and, in the contemplation of Him, self will be forgotten. Love to Christ will be the spring of action. Those who feel the constraining love of God do not ask how little may be given to meet the requirements of God; they do not ask for the lowest standard, but aim at perfect conformity to the will of their Redeemer. With earnest desire they yield all and manifest an interest proportionate to the value of the object which they seek. A profession of Christ without this deep love is mere talk, dry formality, and heavy drudgery.

Do you feel that it is too great a sacrifice to yield all to Christ? Ask yourself the question, "What has Christ given for me?" The Son of God gave all—life and love and suffering—for our redemption. And can it be that we, the unworthy objects of so great love, will withhold our hearts from Him? Every moment of our lives we have been partakers of the blessings of His grace; and, for this very reason, we cannot fully realize the depths of ignorance and misery from which we have been saved. Can we look upon Him whom our sins have pierced, and yet be willing to do despite to all His love and sacrifice? In view of the infinite humiliation of the Lord of glory, shall we murmur because we can enter into life only through conflict and self-abasement?

The inquiry of many a proud heart is, "Why need I go in penitence and humiliation before I can have the assurance of my acceptance with God?" I point you to Christ. He was sinless and, more than this, He was the Prince of heaven; but, in man's behalf, He became sin for the race. "He was numbered with the transgressors; and He bare the sin of many, and made intercession for the transgressors." *Isaiah 53:12.*

What Do We Really Give Up?

But what do we give up, when we give all? A sin-polluted heart, for Jesus to purify, to cleanse by His own blood, and to save by His matchless love. And yet men think it hard to give up all! I am ashamed to hear it spoken of, ashamed to write it.

God does not require us to give up anything that it is for our best interest to retain. In all that He does, He has the well-being of His children in view. Would that all who have not chosen Christ might realize that He has something vastly better to offer them than they are seeking for themselves. Man is doing the greatest injury and injustice to his own soul when he thinks and acts contrary to the will of God. No real joy can be found in the path forbidden by Him who knows what is best and who plans for the good of His creatures. The path of transgression is the path of misery and destruction.

It is a mistake to entertain the thought that God is pleased to see His children suffer. All heaven is interested in the happiness of man. Our heavenly Father does not close the avenues of joy to any of His creatures. The divine requirements call upon us to shun those indulgences that would bring suffering and disappointment, that would close to us the door of happiness and heaven. The world's Redeemer accepts men as they are, with all their wants, imperfections, and weaknesses; and He will not only cleanse from sin and grant redemption through His blood, but will satisfy the heart-longing of all who consent to wear His yoke, to bear His burden. It is His purpose to impart peace and rest to all who come to

Him for the bread of life. He requires us to perform only those duties that will lead our steps to heights of bliss to which the disobedient can never attain. The true, joyous life of the soul is to have Christ formed within, the hope of glory.

How Can I Make the Surrender?

Many are inquiring, "How am I to make the surrender of myself to God?" You desire to give yourself to Him, but you are weak in moral power, in slavery to doubt, and controlled by the habits of your life of sin. Your promises and resolutions are like ropes of sand. You cannot control your thoughts, your impulses, your affections. The knowledge of your broken promises and forfeited pledges weakens your confidence in your own sincerity, and causes you to feel that God cannot accept you; but you need not despair. What you need to understand is the true force of the will. This is the governing power in the nature of man, the power of decision or of choice. Everything depends on the right action of the will. The power of choice God has given to men; it is theirs to exercise. You cannot change your heart, you cannot of yourself give to God its affections; but you can choose to serve Him. You can give Him your will; He will then work in you to will and to do according to His good pleasure. Thus your whole nature will be brought under the control of the Spirit of Christ. Your affections will be centered upon Him; your thoughts will be in harmony with Him.

Desires for goodness and holiness are right as far as they go; but if you stop here, they will avail nothing. Many will be lost while hoping and desiring to be Christians. They do not come to the point of yielding the will to God. They do not now choose to be Christians.

Through the right exercise of the will, an entire change may be made in your life. By yielding up your will to Christ, you ally yourself with the power that is above all principalities and powers. You will have strength from above to hold you steadfast; and thus, through constant surrender to God, you will be enabled to live the new life, even the life of faith.

The Lord heareth the poor. — Psalm 69:33

CHAPTER SIX

By Faith, A New Birth

A girl was sent to a finishing school by her wealthy parents, for they wanted her to have the best that this world offered. There she learned art, dancing, and other "proper" things. But one night she went to an evangelistic meeting, and at the close of the service accepted Christ as her personal Saviour and decided that she would dedicate her life to missionary service.

Writing home to her father, she told him of her decision. He was enraged and immediately wrote back: "Get on the next train and come home immediately."

Upon her arrival home, he told her, "I did not send you to school to get religion. That is all right for poor folk and half-wits, but not for a child in your level of society. You will have to get this religious notion out of your head. ***If by tomorrow morning you have not decided to give up this foolish idea of religion, you may pack your suitcase and leave this home."***

She went to her room with a heavy heart. It meant the loss of love, prestige and wealth,—but most of all, of her parents,—but her decision was made. She cried to the Lord that night and rededicated her life to Him; and very early the next morning she was up and quickly packed her suitcase.

Downstairs, just before leaving, she stepped over to

the piano and started to play and sing:

Jesus, I my cross have taken,
All to leave and follow Thee;
Destitute, despised, forsaken,
Thou, from hence, my all must be:
Perish every fond ambition,
All I've sought and hoped and known;
Yet how rich is my condition,
God and Heav'n are still my own!

She arose and with tears streaming down her face, turned toward the door. Before she could open it, her father stepped out from behind the curtain where he had been listening, and with strong emotion said:

"Wait! I did not know that Jesus Christ meant as much to you as that. I did not know that you were willing to give up father, mother, home and prestige just for Jesus.

Daughter, forgive me. I must be beside myself.
If such a great love can take hold of your heart, there must be something in it. Sit here, please! and tell me how I can be a Christian!"

By faith we accept Christ and a new life begins. And it is a sweet experience. By faith, we walk hand in hand with Him here on earth, awaiting that day when, at His Second Advent, He will return for His own. Then we shall see Him face to face, and, oh, what happiness will be ours!

A mechanic can take material worth six dollars and make an article worth sixty, and we call that skill. An artist can take a piece of canvas worth a dollar, and paint upon it a scene worth a thousand, and we call that art.
But Jesus Christ can reach down and take your life and give forgiveness and obedience—and eternal life. We call that salvation.

Acceptance—through faith—of His plan for your life can bring that wonderful future to you also. Let Him come in, just now.

As your conscience has been quickened by the Holy Spirit, you have seen something of the evil of sin, of its power, its guilt, its woe; and you look upon it with abhorrence. You feel that sin has separated you from God, that you are in bondage to the power of evil. The more you struggle to escape, the more you realize your helplessness. Your motives are impure; your heart is unclean. You see that your life has been filled with selfishness and sin. You long to be forgiven, to be cleansed, to be set free. Harmony with God, likeness to Him—what can you do to obtain it?

It is peace that you need—Heaven's forgiveness and peace and love in the soul. Money cannot buy it, intellect cannot procure it, wisdom cannot attain to it; you can never hope, by your own efforts, to secure it. But God offers it to you as a gift, "without money and without price" (*Isaiah 55:1*). It is yours if you will but reach out your hand and grasp it. The Lord says, "Though your sins be as scarlet, they shall be as white as snow; though they be red like crimson, they shall be as wool." *Isaiah 1:18.* "A new heart also will I give you, and a new spirit will I put within you." *Ezekiel 36:26.*

You have confessed your sins, and in heart put them away. You have resolved to give yourself to God. Now go to Him, and ask that He will wash away your sins and give you a new heart. Then believe that He does this because He has promised. This is the lesson which Jesus taught while He was on earth, that the gift which God promises us we must believe we do receive, and it is ours. Jesus healed the people of their diseases when they had faith in His power; He helped them in the things which they could see, thus inspiring them with confidence in Him concerning things which they could not see—leading them to believe in His power to forgive sins. This He plainly stated in the healing of the man sick with palsy: "That ye may know that the Son of man hath power on earth to forgive sins. Then saith He to the sick of the palsy, Arise, take up thy bed, and go unto thine house." *Matthew 9:6.* So also John the evangelist says, speaking of the miracles of Christ, "These are written, that ye might believe that Jesus is the Christ, the Son of God; and that believing ye might have life through His name." *John 20:31.*

How to Receive Forgiveness

From the simple Bible account of how Jesus healed the sick, we may learn something about how to believe in Him for the forgiveness of sins. Let us turn to the story of the paralytic at Bethesda. The poor sufferer was helpless; he had not used his limbs for thirty-eight years. Yet Jesus bade him, "Rise, take up thy bed, and walk." The sick man might have said, "Lord, if Thou wilt make me whole, I will obey Thy word." But, no, he believed Christ's word, believed that he was made whole, and he made the effort at once; he willed to walk, and he did walk. He acted on the word of Christ, and God gave the power. He was made whole.

In like manner you are a sinner. You cannot atone for your past sins; you cannot change your heart and make yourself holy. But God promises to do all this for you through Christ. You believe that promise. You confess your sins and give yourself to God. You will to serve Him. Just as surely as you do this, God will fulfill His word to you. If you believe the promise,—believe that you are forgiven and cleansed,—God supplies the fact; you are made whole, just as Christ gave the paralytic power to walk when the man believed that he was healed. It is so if you believe it.

Do not wait to feel that you are made whole, but say, "I believe it; it is so, not because I feel it, but because God has promised."

Jesus says, "What things soever ye desire, when ye pray, believe that ye receive them, and ye shall have them." *Mark 11:24.* There is a condition to this promise—that we pray according to the will of God. But it is the will of God to cleanse us from sin, to make us His children, and to enable us to live a holy life. So we may ask for these blessings, and believe that we receive them, and thank God that we have received them. It is our privilege to go to Jesus and be cleansed, and to stand before the law without shame or remorse. "There is therefore now no condemnation to them which are in Christ Jesus, who walk not after the flesh, but after the Spirit." *Romans 8:1.*

A New Life in Christ

Henceforth you are not your own; you are bought with a price. "Ye were not redeemed with corruptible things, as silver and gold; . . but with the precious blood of Christ, as of a lamb without blemish and without spot." *1 Peter 1:18-19.* Through this simple act of believing God, the Holy Spirit has begotten a new life in your heart. You are as a child born into the family of God, and He loves you as He loves His Son.

Now that you have given yourself to Jesus, do not draw back, do not take yourself away from Him, but day by day say, "I am Christ's; I have given myself to Him;" and ask Him to give you His Spirit and keep you by His grace. As it is by giving yourself to God, and believing Him, that you become His child, so you are to live in Him. The apostle says, "As ye have therefore received Christ Jesus the Lord, so walk ye in Him." *Colossians 2:6.*

Some seem to feel that they must be on probation, and must prove to the Lord that they are reformed before they can claim His blessing. But they may claim the blessing of God even now. They must have His grace, the Spirit of Christ, to help their infirmities, or they cannot resist evil. Jesus loves to have us come to Him just as we are, sinful, helpless, dependent. We may come with all our weakness, our folly, our sinfulness, and fall at His feet in penitence. It is His glory to encircle us in the arms of His love and to bind up our wounds, to cleanse us from all impurity.

They Do Not Believe

Here is where thousands fail; they do not believe that Jesus pardons them personally, individually. They do not take God at His word. It is the privilege of all who comply with the conditions, to know for themselves that pardon is freely extended for every sin. Put away the suspicion that God's promises are not meant for you. They are for every repentant transgressor. Strength and grace have been provided through Christ to be brought by ministering angels to every believing soul. None are so sinful that they cannot find strength, purity, and righteousness in Jesus, who died for them. He is waiting to strip them of their garments, stained and polluted with sin, and to put upon them the white robes of righteousness; He bids them live and not die.

God does not deal with us as finite men deal with one another. His thoughts are thoughts of mercy, love, and tenderest compassion. He says, "Let the wicked forsake his way, and the unrighteous man his thoughts: and let him return unto the Lord, and He will have mercy upon him; and to our God, for He will abundantly pardon" (*Isaiah 55:7*). "I have blotted out, as a thick cloud, thy transgressions, and, as a cloud, thy sins." *Isaiah 44:22.*

"I have no pleasure in the death of him that dieth, saith the Lord God: wherefore turn yourselves, and live ye." *Ezekiel 18:32.* Satan is ready to steal away the blessed assurances of God. He desires to take every glimmer of hope and every ray of light from the soul; but you must not permit him to do this. Do not give ear to the tempter, but say, "Jesus has died that I might live. He loves me and wills not that I should perish. I have a compassionate heavenly Father; and although I have abused His love, though the blessings He has given me have been squandered, I will arise, and go to my Father, and say, 'I have sinned against heaven and before Thee, and am no more worthy to be called Thy son: make me as one of Thy hired servants.' " The parable tells you how the wanderer will be received: "When he was yet a great way off, his father saw him, and had compassion, and ran, and fell on his neck, and kissed him." *Luke 15:18-20.*

Drawn to Him by Love

But even this parable, tender and touching as it is, comes short of expressing the infinite compassion of the heavenly Father. The Lord declares by His prophet, "I have loved thee with an everlasting love: therefore with loving-kindness have I drawn thee." *Jeremiah 31:3.* While the sinner is yet far from the Father's house, wasting his substance in a strange country, the Father's heart is yearning over him; and every longing awakened in the soul to return to God is but the tender pleading of His Spirit, wooing, entreating, drawing the wanderer to his Father's heart of love.

With the rich promises of the Bible before you, can you give place to doubt? Can you believe that when the poor sinner longs to return, longs to forsake his sins, the Lord sternly withholds him from coming to His feet in repentance? Away with such thoughts! Nothing can hurt your own soul more than to entertain such a conception of our heavenly Father. He hates sin, but He loves the sinner; and He gave Himself in the person of Christ, that all who would might be saved and have eternal blessedness in the kingdom of glory. What stronger or more tender language could have been employed than He has chosen in which to express His love toward us? He declares, "Can a woman forget her sucking child, that she should not have compassion on the son of her womb? yea, they may forget, yet will I not forget thee." *Isaiah 49:15.*

Look Up and Come

Look up, you that are doubting and trembling; for Jesus lives to make intercession for us. Thank God for the gift of His dear Son and pray that He may not have died for you in vain. The Spirit invites you today. Come with your whole heart to Jesus, and you may claim His blessing.

As you read the promises, remember they are the expression of unutterable love and pity. The great heart of Infinite Love is drawn toward the sinner with boundless compassion. "We have redemption through His blood, the forgiveness of sins." *Ephesians 1:7.* Yes, only believe that God is your helper. He wants to restore His moral image in man. As you draw near to Him with confession and repentance, He will draw near to you with mercy and forgiveness.

When thou art in tribulation,
And all these things are come upon thee,
Even in the latter days,
If thou turn to the Lord thy God,
And shalt be obedient unto His voice:
For the Lord thy God is a merciful God,
He will not forsake thee.
— Deuteronomy 4:30-31

BIBLE PROMISES YOU CAN USE

I have set the Lord always before me; because He is at my right hand, I shall not be moved. *– Psalm 16:8.*

He shall not be afraid of evil tidings; his heart is fixed, trusting in the Lord. *– Psalm 112:7.*

I will both lay me down in peace and sleep; for Thou, Lord, only makest me dwell in safety. *– Psalm 4:8.*

He giveth His beloved sleep. *– Psalm 127:2.*

The beloved of the Lord shall dwell in safety by Him: and the Lord shall cover him all the day long. *– Deuteronomy 33:12.*

The Lord is my light and my salvation; whom shall I fear? The Lord is the strength of my life; of whom shall I be afraid? *– Psalm 27:1 .*

He that dwelleth in the secret place of the Most High shall abide under the shadow of the Almighty. *– Psalm 91:1.*

My help cometh from the Lord, which made heaven and earth . . Behold, He that keepeth Israel shall neither slumber nor sleep. *– Psalm 121:2, 4.*

But whoso hearkeneth unto Me shall dwell safely, and shall be quiet from fear of evil. *– Proverbs 1:33.*

When thou passest through the waters, I will be with thee; and through the rivers, they shall not overflow thee. *– Isaiah 43:2.*

The Lord will give strength unto His people; the Lord will bless His people with peace. *– Psalm 29:11.*

Great peace have they which love Thy Law, and nothing shall offend them. *– Psalm 119:165.*

The steps of a good man are ordered by the Lord; and he delighteth in His way. *– Psalm 37:23.*

Trust in the Lord with all thine heart; and lean not unto thine own understanding. In all thy ways acknowledge Him, and He shall direct thy paths. *– Proverbs 3:5-6.*

I will bring the blind by a way that they knew not; I will lead them in paths that they have not known. I will make darkness light before them, and crooked things straight. These things will I do unto them, and not forsake them. *–Isaiah 42:16.*

Them that honour Me I will honour. *– 1 Samuel 2:30.*

CHAPTER SEVEN

Obeying Him

Ignace Paderewski (1860-1941) was one of the greatest pianists that ever lived. When he came onto the stage, a hushed silence fell over the audience, a hush that lasted until he left. No one hearing one of his performances ever forgot it. When he died, a world mourned.

What made Paderewski different from you or me? "Well," one might say, "It was his genius." Another could add, "It was his dedication. "A third could say, "He had more music in his heart than the rest of us have."

If I were to try to play upon a piano that Paderewski had just finished performing on, the contrast would be most painful. I could bang on it all I desired, but would be unable to produce anything that even a child could appreciate.

We live today in a world in which people want liberty more than obedience to laws. It is claimed that liberty can bring freedom which submission to rules could never accomplish. Such talk is even to be heard in many of the pulpits of the land. It is said that even the God of heaven has no laws that man must obey. Yet every schoolboy knows that every earthly government has laws, and that men must obey those laws. Our world would be in total anarchy if men did not obey governmental laws.

The God of heaven and earth has laws also. He has

physical laws and moral laws that must ever govern His creatures. Without obedience to His laws, mankind can never truly be happy. Indeed, when men refuse to obey the laws of God, they ultimately destroy themselves.

And now, more clearly, we can understand Paderewski. His towering craftsmanship was more than deep feeling and agile fingers. And it was more than liberty.

I have perfect liberty when I sit at the piano—but I accomplish nothing there.

Liberty cannot produce a highly trained musician—only obedience can! When I sit at the piano, liberty accomplishes little, for it is not controlled by submission to the laws that govern melody, harmony, rhythm, tempo and counterpoint.

Those Christians who are the closest to God are the ones who have yielded the most to the guidance of His Holy Spirit and, through faith in His Son, have obeyed the Holy Scriptures and the Ten Commandments. It is God's work—through Christ—to save us from sin, not in sin.

And it is our work, through faith in Christ, to cooperate with His plan for our lives.

The will of God is a pure, clean, obedient life for each of His little children. And this is what you and I want also, is it not?

Why did Jesus have to die? Because man had sinned, and "sin is the transgression of the law" (1 John 3:4). If the Ten Commandments could have been set aside or abolished, then Christ would not have had to die. But to do away with the moral standard would be to effectually do away with morality! Jesus died because the Moral Law could not be done away with. He died, not to abolish the law, but to enable men to keep it.

Thank God, all your life, that His grace is so powerful it can enable you to control yourself. By faith in Christ's empowering merits, you can be strengthened, moment by moment, to obey all that He asks in His Holy Word.

"If any man be in Christ, he is a new creature: old things are passed away; behold, all things are become new." 2 *Corinthians 5:17.*

A person may not be able to tell the exact time or place, or trace all the chain of circumstances in the process of conversion; but this does not prove him to be unconverted. Christ said to Nicodemus, "The wind bloweth where it listeth, and thou hearest the sound thereof, but canst not tell whence it cometh, and whither it goeth: so is everyone that is born of the Spirit." *John 3:8.* Like the wind, which is invisible, yet the effects of which are plainly seen and felt, is the Spirit of God in its work upon the human heart. That regenerating power, which no human eye can see, begets a new life in the soul; it creates a new being in the image of God. While the work of the Spirit is silent and imperceptible, its effects are manifest. If the heart has been renewed by the Spirit of God, the life will bear witness to the fact. While we cannot do anything to change our hearts or to bring ourselves into harmony with God; while we must not trust at all to ourselves or our good works, our lives will reveal whether the grace of God is dwelling within us. A change will be seen in the character, the habits, the pursuits. The contrast will be clear and decided between what they have been and what they are. The character is revealed, not by occasional good deeds and occasional misdeeds, but by the tendency of the habitual words and acts.

It is true that there may be an outward correctness of deportment without the renewing power of Christ. The love of influence and the desire for the esteem of others may produce a well-ordered life. Self-respect may lead us to avoid the appearance of evil. A selfish heart may perform generous actions. By what means, then, shall we determine whose side we are on?

Who has the heart? With whom are our thoughts? Of whom do we love to converse? Who has our warmest affections and our best energies? If we are Christ's, our thoughts are with Him, and our sweetest thoughts are of Him. All we have and are is consecrated to Him. We long to bear His image, breathe His spirit, do His will, and please Him in all things.

New Creatures with New Fruit

Those who become new creatures in Christ Jesus will bring forth the fruits of the Spirit, "love, joy, peace, long-suffering, gentleness, goodness, faith, meekness, temperance." *Galatians 5:22-23.* They will no longer fashion themselves according to the former lusts; but, by the faith of the Son of God, they will follow in His steps, reflect His character, and purify themselves even as He is pure. The things they once hated they now love, and the things they once loved they hate. The proud and self-assertive become meek and lowly in heart. The vain and supercilious become serious and unobtrusive. The drunken becomes sober, and the profligate pure. The vain customs and fashions of the world are laid aside. Christians will seek not the "outward adorning," but "the hidden man of the heart, in that which is not corruptible, even the ornament of a meek and quiet spirit" (*1 Peter 3:3-4*).

There is no evidence of genuine repentance unless it works reformation. If he restore the pledge, give again that he had robbed, confess his sins, and love God and his fellow men, the sinner may be sure that he has passed from death unto life.

When, as erring, sinful beings, we come to Christ and become partakers of His pardoning grace, love springs up in the heart. Every burden is light, for the yoke that Christ imposes is easy. Duty becomes a delight and sacrifice a pleasure. The path that before seemed shrouded in darkness becomes bright with beams from the Sun of Righteousness.

The loveliness of the character of Christ will be seen in His followers. It was His delight to do the will of God. Love to God, zeal for His glory, was the controlling power in our Saviour's life. Love beautified and ennobled all His actions. Love is of God. The unconsecrated heart cannot originate or produce it. It is found only in the heart where Jesus reigns. "We love because He first loved us." *1 John 4:19* In the heart renewed by divine grace, love is the principle of action. It modifies the character, governs the impulses, controls the passions, subdues enmity, and ennobles the affections. This love, cherished in the soul, sweetens the life and sheds a refining influence on all around.

Two Errors

There are two errors against which the children of God—particularly those who have just come to trust in His grace—especially need to guard. The first, already dwelt upon, is that of looking to their own works, trusting to anything they can do, to bring themselves into harmony with God. He who is trying to become holy by his own works in keeping the law, is attempting an impossibility. All that man can do without Christ is polluted with selfishness and sin. It is the grace of Christ alone, through faith, that can make us holy.

The opposite and no less dangerous error is that belief in Christ releases men from keeping the law of God; that since by faith alone we become partakers of the grace of Christ, our works have nothing to do with our redemption.

But notice here that obedience is not a mere outward compliance, but the service of love. The law of God is an expression of His very nature; it is an embodiment of the great principle of love, and hence is the foundation of His government in heaven and earth. If our hearts are renewed in the likeness of God, if the divine love is implanted in the soul, will not the law of God be carried out in the life? When the principle of love is implanted in the heart, when man is renewed after the image of Him that created him, the new-covenant promise is fulfilled, "I will put My laws into their hearts, and in their minds will I write them." *Hebrews 10:16.* And if the law is written in the heart, will it not shape the life? Obedience—the service and allegiance of love—is the true sign of discipleship. Thus the Scripture says, "This is the love of God, that we keep His commandments." *1 John 5:3.* "He that saith, I know Him, and keepeth not His commandments, is a liar, and the truth is not in him." *1 John 2:4.* Instead of releasing man from obedience, it is faith, and faith only, that makes us partakers of the grace of Christ, which enables us to render obedience.

Obedience Is the Test

We do not earn salvation by our obedience; for salvation is the free gift of God, to be received by faith. But obedience is the fruit of faith. "Ye know that He was manifested to take away our sins; and in Him is no sin. Whosoever abideth in Him sinneth not: whosoever sinneth hath not seen Him, neither known Him." *1 John 3:5-6*. Here is the true test. If we abide in Christ, if the love of God dwells in us, our feelings, our thoughts, our purposes, our actions, will be in harmony with the will of God as expressed in the precepts of His holy law. "Little children, let no man deceive you: he that doeth righteousness is righteous, even as He is righteous." *1 John 3:7*. Righteousness is defined by the standard of God's holy law, as expressed in the ten precepts given on Sinai.

That so-called faith in Christ which professes to release men from the obligation of obedience to God, is not faith, but presumption. "By grace are ye saved through faith." *Ephesians 2:8*. But "faith, if it hath not works, is dead." *James 2:17*. Jesus said of Himself before He came to earth, "I delight to do Thy will, O My God: yea, Thy law is within My heart." *Psalm 40:8*. And just before He ascended again to heaven He declared, "I have kept My Father's commandments, and abide in His love." *John 15:10*. The Scripture says, "Hereby we do know that we know Him, if we keep His commandments . . He that saith he abideth in Him ought himself also so to walk even as He walked." *1 John 2:3, 6*. "Because Christ also suffered for us, leaving us an example, that ye should follow His steps." *1 Peter 2:21*.

Living like Jesus

The condition of eternal life is now just what it always has been,—just what it was in Paradise before the fall of our first parents,—perfect obedience to the law of God, perfect righteousness. If eternal life were granted on any condition short of this, then the happiness of the whole universe would be imperiled. The way would be open for sin, with all its train of woe and misery, to be immortalized.

It was possible for Adam, before the fall, to form a righteous character by obedience to God's law. But he failed to do this, and because of his sin our natures are fallen and we cannot make ourselves righteous. Since we are sinful, unholy, we cannot perfectly obey the holy law. We have no righteousness of our own with which to meet the claims of the law of God. But Christ has made a way of escape for us. He lived on earth amid trials and temptations such as we have to meet. He lived a sinless life. He died for us, and now He offers to take our sins and give us His righteousness. If you give yourself to Him, and accept Him as your Saviour, then, sinful as your life may have been, for His sake you are accounted righteous. Christ's character stands in place of your character, and you are accepted before God just as if you had not sinned.

Victory through Christ

More than this, Christ changes the heart. He abides in your heart by faith. You are to maintain this connection with Christ by faith and the continual surrender of your will to Him; and, so long as you do this, He will work in you to will and to do according to His good pleasure. So you may say, "The life which I now live in the flesh I live by the faith of the Son of God, who loved me, and gave Himself for me." *Galatians 2:20*. So Jesus said to His disciples, "It is not ye that speak, but the Spirit of your Father which speaketh in you." *Matthew 10:20*. Then with Christ working in you, you will manifest the same spirit and do the same good works—works of righteousness, obedience.

So we have nothing in ourselves of which to boast. We have no ground for self-exaltation. Our only ground of hope is in the righteousness of Christ imputed to us, and in that wrought by His Spirit working in and through us.

When we speak of faith, there is a distinction that should be borne in mind. There is a kind of belief that is wholly distinct from faith. The existence and power of God, the truth of His Word, are facts that even Satan and his hosts cannot at heart deny. The Bible says that "the devils also believe, and tremble," but this is not faith. *James 2:19*. Where there is not only a belief in God's Word, but a submission of the will to Him; where the heart is yielded to Him, the affections fixed upon Him, there is faith—faith that works by love and purifies the soul. Through this faith the heart is renewed in the image of God. And the heart that in its unrenewed state is not subject to the law of God, neither indeed can be, now delights in its holy precepts, exclaiming with the psalmist, "O how love I Thy law! It is my meditation all the day." *Psalm 119:97*. And the righteousness of the law is fulfilled in us, "who walk not after the flesh, but after the Spirit." *Romans 8:1*.

Keep Coming Back

There are those who have known the pardoning love of Christ and who really desire to be children of God, yet they realize that their character is imperfect, their life faulty, and they are ready to doubt whether their hearts have been renewed by the Holy Spirit. To such I would say, Do not draw back in despair. We shall often have to bow down and weep at the feet of Jesus because of our shortcomings and mistakes, but we are not to be discouraged. Even if we are overcome by the enemy, we are not cast off, not forsaken and rejected of God. No; Christ is at the right hand of God, who also maketh intercession for us. Said the beloved John, "These things write I unto you, that ye sin not. And if any man sin, we have an advocate with the Father, Jesus Christ the righteous." *1 John 2:1*. And do not forget the words of Christ, "The Father Himself loveth you." *John 16:27*. He desires to restore you to Himself, to see His own purity and holiness reflected in you. And if you will but yield yourself to Him, He that hath begun a good work in you will carry it forward to the day of Jesus Christ. Pray more fervently; believe more fully. As we come to distrust our own power, let us trust the power of our Redeemer, and we shall praise Him who is the health of our countenance.

The closer you come to Jesus, the more faulty you will appear in your own eyes; for your vision will be clearer, and your imperfections will be seen in broad and distinct contrast to His perfect nature. This is evidence that Satan's delusions have lost their power; that the vivifying influence of the Spirit of God is arousing you.

Knowing God and Ourselves

No deep-seated love for Jesus can dwell in the heart that does not realize its own sinfulness. The soul that is transformed by the grace of Christ will admire His divine character; but if we do not see our own moral deformity, it is unmistakable evidence that we have not had a view of the beauty and excellence of Christ.

The less we see to esteem in ourselves, the more we shall see to esteem in the infinite purity and loveliness of our Saviour. A view of our sinfulness drives us to Him who can pardon; and when the soul, realizing its helplessness, reaches out after Christ, He will reveal Himself in power. The more our sense of need drives us to Him and to the Word of God, the more exalted views we shall have of His character, and the more fully we shall reflect His image.

If we confess our sins,
He is faithful and just to forgive us our sins;
And to cleanse us
From all unrighteousness.
— 1 John 1:9

He that covereth his sins
Shall not prosper;
But whoso confesseth and forsaketh them
Shall have mercy.
— Proverbs 28:13

I beseech you therefore, brethren,
By the mercies of God,
That ye present your bodies
A living sacrifice,
Holy, acceptable unto God,
Which is your reasonable service.
— Romans 12:1

BIBLE PROMISES YOU CAN USE

For this God is our God for ever and ever: He will be our guide even unto death. *– Psalm 48:14.*

Because he hath set his love upon Me, therefore will I deliver him; . . He shall call upon Me, and I will answer him. I will be with him in trouble; I will deliver him and honor him. *– Psalm 91:14-15.*

If any man serve Me, let him follow Me; and where I am, there shall also my servant be. If any man serve Me, him will My Father honor. *– John 12:26.*

But his delight is in the Law of the Lord; and in His Law doth he meditate day and night. And he shall be like a tree planted by the rivers of water. *– Psalm 1:2-3.*

Commit thy way unto the Lord; trust also in Him, and He shall bring it to pass. *– Psalm 37:5.*

I will cry unto God most high; unto God, that performeth all things for me. *– Psalm 57:2.*

Better is little with the fear of the Lord than great treasure and trouble therewith. *– Proverbs 15:16.*

Thou shalt keep His statutes . . that it may go well with thee, and with thy children after thee. *– Deuteronomy 4:40.*

In the fear of the Lord is strong confidence; and His children shall have a place of refuge. *– Proverbs 14:26.*

I have been young, and now am old; yet have I not seen the righteous forsaken, nor his seed begging bread. He is ever merciful and lendeth. *– Psalm 37:25-26.*

He hath blessed thy children with thee. *– Psalm 147:13.*

Thou art my hiding place; Thou shalt preserve me from trouble; Thou shalt compass me about with songs of deliverance. *– Psalm 32:7.*

The Lord preserveth the faithful. *– Psalm 31:23.*

There shall no evil befall thee, neither shall any plague come nigh thy dwelling. *– Psalm 91:10.*

The way of the righteous is made plain. *–Proverbs 15:19.*

In His favor is life; weeping may endure for a night, but joy cometh in the morning. *– Psalm 30:5.*

Many are the afflictions of the righteous; but the Lord delivereth him out of them all. *– Psalm 34:19.*

CHAPTER EIGHT

Abiding in Him

At the foot of the Kaylass Mountains there is a district which is full of sweet-scented flowers. One day as Sadhu Sundar Singh was traveling through on his way to the East, he began walking through an area several miles in length, which contained fields of these flowers.

He relates that their beauty and fragrance gave him great pleasure, and he finally stopped to rest among them. Just then a man, coming out of the jungle, called out, "You must not stop here; this is a place of great danger. Many have died here."

Very surprised, Sundar Singh asked, "Are there deadly serpents here or robbers?"

The answer was full of meaning: "If you take in the scent of these flowers for a time, sleep will overpower you. And once asleep, it will be difficult for anyone to awaken you. Some have been known to sleep in this way for ten or twelve days, and it ends in death."

Here was a beautiful flower that appeared totally harmless to the gaze and even to the touch. But its aroma first imparts a false restfulness, and then a sleep of death. In this life, we must come to Christ, cry to Christ, cling to Christ, and work with Christ—or we shall return to our sins.

Many who have come to Christ return to the pleasures of the world, and do not realize what they have done. They imagine that they are still Christians, when in most of their ways they are only living for themselves and this world.

Dr. Drummond writes of the African white ant that eats the heart out of structures, in a manner strikingly similar to the way in which sin eats the heart out of human lives.

"One may never see the insect, for it lives underground, but its ravages confront one at every turn in the heart of Central Africa.

"You can select a site and build your house, and for a few months fancy that you have pitched upon the one solitary place in the country where there are no white ants. But one day the doorpost suddenly totters, and if you do not move out hurriedly—the lintel and rafters will shortly thereafter come down with a crash over your head.

"Picking up a piece of the wrecked timbers, you examine it and discover that the whole inside has been eaten away! The walls and ceiling of your once-sturdy house have become worthless husks, and the apparently solid logs in the floor and foundation, that everything was built on,—have become mere cylinders of bark. Through most of them you can now push your thumb."

The secret is in a day-by-day abiding in Christ. Remaining by His side, we are secure.

"By faith in Him as a personal Saviour the union is formed. The sinner unites his weakness to Christ's . . enduring might . . This union with Christ, once formed, must be maintained. Christ said, 'Abide in Me, and I in you. As the branch cannot bear fruit of itself, except it abide in the vine; no more can ye, except ye abide in Me.' This is no casual touch, no off-and-on connection. The branch becomes a part of the living vine . . Separated from the vine, the branch cannot live."

—*Desire of Ages, pages 675-676.*

The change of heart by which we become children of God is, in the Bible, spoken of as birth. Again, it is compared to the germination of the good seed sown by the husbandman. In like manner those who are just converted to Christ are, "as newborn babes" (*1 Peter 2:2*), to "grow up" (*Ephesians 4:15*) to the stature of men and women in Christ Jesus. Or like the good seed sown in the field, they are to grow up and bring forth fruit. Isaiah says that they shall "be called trees of righteousness, the planting of the Lord, that He might be glorified." *Isaiah 61:3*. So from natural life, illustrations are drawn, to help us better to understand the mysterious truths of spiritual life.

Not all the wisdom and skill of man can produce life in the smallest object in nature. It is only through the life which God Himself has imparted, that either plant or animal can live. So it is only through the life from God that spiritual life is begotten in the hearts of men. Unless a man is "born from above," he cannot become a partaker of the life which Christ came to give (*John 3:3, margin*).

As with life, so it is with growth. It is God who brings the bud to bloom and the flower to fruit. It is by His power that the seed develops, "first the blade, then the ear, after that the full corn in the ear" (*Mark 4:28*). And the prophet, Hosea, says of Israel, that "he shall grow as the lily . . They shall revive as the corn, and grow as the vine." *Hosea 14:5, 7*. And Jesus bids us "consider the lilies how they grow." *Luke 12:27*. The plants and flowers grow not by their own care or anxiety or effort, but by receiving that which God has furnished to minister to their life. The child cannot, by any anxiety or power of its own, add to its stature. No more can you, by anxiety or effort of yourself, secure spiritual growth. The plant, the child, grows by receiving from its surroundings that which ministers to its life—air, sunshine, and food. What these gifts of nature are to animal and plant, such is Christ to those who trust in Him. He is their "everlasting light" (*Isaiah 60:19*), "a sun and shield" (*Psalm 84:11*). He shall be as "the dew unto Israel" (*Hosea 14:5*). "He shall come down like rain upon the mown grass." *Psalm*

72:6. He is the living water, "the Bread of God . . which cometh down from heaven, and giveth life unto the world" (*John 6:33*).

Choosing Life

In the matchless gift of His Son, God has encircled the whole world with an atmosphere of grace as real as the air which circulates around the globe. All who choose to breathe this life-giving atmosphere will live and grow up to the stature of men and women in Christ Jesus.

As the flower turns to the sun, that the bright beams may aid in perfecting its beauty and symmetry, so should we turn to the Sun of Righteousness, that heaven's light may shine upon us, that our character may be developed into the likeness of Christ.

Jesus teaches the same thing when He says, "Abide in Me, and I in you. As the branch cannot bear fruit of itself, except it abide in the vine; no more can ye, except ye abide in Me . . Without Me ye can do nothing." *John 15:4-5*. You are just as dependent upon Christ, in order to live a holy life, as is the branch upon the parent stock for growth and fruitfulness. Apart from Him you have no life. You have no power to resist temptation or to grow in grace and holiness. Abiding in Him, you may flourish. Drawing your life from Him, you will not wither nor be fruitless. You will be like a tree planted by the rivers of water.

Many have an idea that they must do some part of the work alone. They have trusted in Christ for the forgiveness of sin, but now they seek by their own efforts to live aright. But every such effort must fail. Jesus says, "Without Me ye can do nothing." Our growth in grace, our joy, our usefulness,—all depend upon our union with Christ. It is by communion with Him, daily, hourly,—by abiding in Him,—that we are to grow in grace. He is not only the Author, but the Finisher of our faith. It is Christ first and last and always. He is to be with us, not only at the beginning and the end of our course, but at every step of the way. David says, "I have set the Lord always before me: because He is at my right hand, I shall not be moved." *Psalm 16:8*.

Come - and Give - and Take

Do you ask, "How am I to abide in Christ?" In the same way as you received Him at first. "As ye have therefore received Christ Jesus the Lord, so walk ye in Him." *Colossians 2:6*. "The just shall live by faith." *Hebrews 10:38.* You gave yourself to God, to be His wholly, to serve and obey Him, and you took Christ as your Saviour. You could not yourself atone for your sins or change your heart; but having given yourself to God, you believe that He, for Christ's sake, did all this for you. By faith you became Christ's, and by faith you are to grow up in Him—by giving and taking. You are to give all,—your heart, your will, your service,—give yourself to Him to obey all His requirements; and you must take all,—Christ, the fullness of all blessing, to abide in your heart, to be your strength, your righteousness, your everlasting helper,—to give you power to obey.

Consecrate yourself to God in the morning; make this your very first work. Let your prayer be, "Take me, O Lord, as wholly Thine. I lay all my plans at Thy feet. Use me today in Thy service. Abide with me, and let all my work be wrought in Thee." This is a daily matter. Each morning consecrate yourself to God for that day. Surrender all your plans to Him, to be carried out or given up as His providence shall indicate. Thus day by day you may be giving your life into the hands of God, and thus your life will be molded more and more after the life of Christ.

A life in Christ is a life of restfulness. There may be no ecstasy of feeling, but there should be an abiding, peaceful trust. Your hope is not in yourself; it is in Christ. Your weakness is united to His strength, your ignorance to His wisdom, your frailty to His enduring might. So you are not to look to yourself, not to let the mind dwell upon self, but look to Christ. Let the mind dwell upon His love, upon the beauty, the perfection, of His character. Christ in His self-denial, Christ in His humiliation, Christ in His purity and holiness, Christ in His matchless love—this is the subject for the soul's contemplation. It is by loving Him, copying Him, depending wholly upon Him, that you are to be transformed into His likeness.

Abiding in Him

Jesus says, "Abide in Me." These words convey the idea of rest, stability, confidence. Again He invites, "Come unto Me, . . and I will give you rest." *Matthew 11:28.* The words of the psalmist express the same thought: "Rest in the Lord, and wait patiently for Him." *Psalm 37:7.* And Isaiah gives the assurance, "In quietness and in confidence shall be your strength." *Isaiah 30:15.* This rest is not found in inactivity; for, in the Saviour's invitation, the promise of rest is united with the call to labor: "Take My yoke upon you: . . and ye shall find rest." *Matthew 11:29.* The heart that rests most fully upon Christ will be most earnest and active in labor for Him.

When the mind dwells upon self, it is turned away from Christ, the source of strength and life. Hence it is Satan's constant effort to keep the attention diverted from the Saviour and thus prevent the union and communion of the soul with Christ. The pleasures of the world, life's cares and perplexities and sorrows, the faults of others, or your own faults and imperfections—to any or all of these he will seek to divert the mind. Do not be misled by his devices. Many who are really conscientious, and who desire to live for God, he too often leads to dwell upon their own faults and weaknesses, and thus by separating them from Christ he hopes to gain the victory. We should not make self the center and indulge anxiety and fear as to whether we shall be saved. All this turns the soul away from the Source of our strength. Commit the keeping of your soul to God, and trust in Him. Talk and think of Jesus. Let self be lost in Him. Put away all doubt; dismiss your fears. Say with the apostle Paul, "I live; yet not I, but Christ liveth in me: and the life which I now live in the flesh I live by the faith of the Son of God, who loved me, and gave Himself for me." *Galatians 2:20.* Rest in God. He is able to keep that which you have committed to Him. If you will leave yourself in His hands, He will bring you off more than conqueror through Him that has loved you.

Only We Can Break the Connection

When Christ took human nature upon Him, He bound humanity to Himself by a tie of love that can never be broken by any power, save the choice of man himself. Satan will constantly present allurements to induce us to break this tie—to choose to separate ourselves from Christ. Here is where we need to watch, to strive, to pray, that nothing may entice us to choose another master; for we are always free to do this. But let us keep our eyes fixed upon Christ, and He will preserve us. Looking unto Jesus, we are safe. Nothing can pluck us out of His hand. In constantly beholding Him, we "are changed into the same image from glory to glory, even as by the Spirit of the Lord." *2 Corinthians 3:18.*

It was thus that the early disciples gained their likeness to the dear Saviour. When those disciples heard the words of Jesus, they felt their need of Him. They sought, they found, they followed Him. They were with Him in the house, at the table, in the closet, in the field. They were with Him as pupils with a teacher, daily receiving from His lips lessons of holy truth. They looked to Him, as servants to their master, to learn their duty. Those disciples were men "subject to like passions as we are" (*James 5:17*). They had the same battle with sin to fight. They needed the same grace, in order to live a holy life.

How it Changed John

Even John, the beloved disciple, the one who most fully reflected the likeness of the Saviour, did not naturally possess that loveliness of character. He was not only self-assertive and ambitious for honor, but impetuous and resentful under injuries. But as the character of the Divine One was manifested to him, he saw his own deficiency and was humbled by the knowledge. The strength and patience, the power and tenderness, the majesty and meekness, that he beheld in the daily life of the Son of God, filled his soul with admiration and love. Day by day his heart was drawn out toward Christ, until he lost sight of self in love for his Master. His resentful, ambitious temper was yielded to the molding power of Christ. The regenerating influence of the Holy

Spirit renewed his heart. The power of the love of Christ wrought a transformation of character. This is the sure result of union with Jesus. When Christ abides in the heart, the whole nature is transformed. Christ's Spirit, His love, softens the heart, subdues the soul, and raises the thoughts and desires toward God and heaven.

When Christ ascended to heaven, the sense of His presence was still with His followers. It was a personal presence, full of love and light. Jesus, the Saviour, who had walked and talked and prayed with them, who had spoken hope and comfort to their hearts, had, while the message of peace was still upon His lips, been taken up from them into heaven, and the tones of His voice had come back to them, as the cloud of angels received Him: "Lo, I am with you alway, even unto the end of the world" (*Matthew 28:20*). He had ascended to heaven in the form of humanity. They knew that He was before the throne of God, their Friend and Saviour still; that His sympathies were unchanged; that He was still identified with suffering humanity. He was presenting before God the merits of His own precious blood, showing His wounded hands and feet, in remembrance of the price He had paid for His redeemed. They knew that He had ascended to heaven to prepare places for them, and that He would come again and take them to Himself.

Extending the Hand Higher

As they met together after the ascension they were eager to present their requests to the Father in the name of Jesus. In solemn awe they bowed in prayer, repeating the assurance, "Whatsoever ye shall ask the Father in My name, He will give it you. Hitherto have ye asked nothing in My name: ask, and ye shall receive, that your joy may be full." *John 16:23-24*. They extended the hand of faith higher and higher with the mighty argument, "It is Christ that died, yea rather, that is risen again, who is even at the right hand of God, who also maketh intercession for us" (*Romans 8:34*). And Pentecost brought them the presence of the Comforter, of whom Christ had said, He "shall be in you" (*John 14:17*). And He had further said, "It is expedient for you that I go away: for if I go not away, the Comforter will not come unto you; but if I depart, I will send Him unto you." *John 16:7*. Henceforth through the Spirit, Christ was to abide continually in the hearts of His children. Their union with Him was closer than when He was personally with them. The light, and love, and power of the indwelling Christ shone out through them, so that men, beholding, "marveled; and they took knowledge of them, that they had been with Jesus" (*Acts 4:13*).

All that Christ was to the disciples, He desires to be to His children today; for in that last prayer, with the little band of disciples gathered about Him, He said, "Neither pray I for these alone, but for them also which shall believe on Me through their word." *John 17:20*.

Jesus prayed for us, and He asked that we might be one with Him, even as He is one with the Father. What a union is this! The Saviour has said of Himself, "The Son can do nothing of Himself" (*John 5:19*); "the Father that dwelleth in Me, He doeth the works" (*John 14:10*). Then if Christ is dwelling in our hearts, He will work in us "both to will and to do of His good pleasure." *Philippians 2:13*. We shall work as He worked; we shall manifest the same spirit. And thus, loving Him and abiding in Him, we shall "grow up into Him in all things, which is the head, even Christ" (*Ephesians 4:15*).

In every thing give thanks:
For this is the will of God
in Christ Jesus Concerning you.
— 1 Thessalonians 5:18

He satisfieth the longing soul,
and filleth the hungry soul with goodness.
— Psalm 107:9

I will bless the Lord at all times:
His praise shall continually
be in my mouth.
— Psalm 34:1

BIBLE PROMISES YOU CAN USE

Why art thou cast down, 0 my soul? and why art thou disquieted within me? Hope thou in God; for I shall yet praise Him, who is the health of my countenance, and my God.
– Psalm 42:11.

Thou wilt save the afflicted people, but wilt bring down high looks. For Thou wilt light my candle: the Lord my God will enlighten my darkness. *– Psalm 18:27-28.*

The Lord openeth the eyes of the blind; the Lord raiseth them that are bowed down. *– Psalm 146:8.*

They cry unto the Lord in their trouble; and He saveth them out of their distresses. *– Psalm 107:19.*

They that sow in tears shall reap in joy. He that goeth forth and weepeth, bearing precious seed, shall doubtless come again with rejoicing, bringing his sheaves with him.
– Psalm 126:5-6.

Their soul shall be as a watered garden, and they shall not sorrow any more . . I will turn their mourning into joy, and will comfort them, and make them rejoice from their sorrow.
– Jeremiah 31:12-13.

The Lord also will be a refuge for the oppressed, a refuge in times of trouble. *– Psalm 9:9.*

Wait on the Lord; be of good courage, and He shall strengthen thy heart. Wait, I say, on the Lord . . When my father and my mother forsake me, then the Lord will take me up.
– Psalm 27:14, 10.

The Lord is my rock, and my fortress, and my deliverer; my God, my strength, in whom I will trust: my buckler, and the horn of my salvation, and my high tower. *– Psalm 18:2.*

God is our refuge and strength, a very present help in trouble. Therefore will not we fear, though the earth be removed, and though the mountains be carried into the midst of the sea; though the waters thereof roar, and be troubled; though the mountains shake with the swelling thereof.
– Psalm 46:1-3.

Thou hast given commandment to save me: for Thou art my rock and my fortress. *– Psalm 71:3.*

CHAPTER NINE

Working with Him

C.T. Studd had been a very wealthy man, but when he found Christ as his Saviour from sin, he then totally dedicated his life to the One who died that he might have eternal life.

Leaving his native England, he went by ship to China. There he worked, year after year, to bring lost souls to a knowledge of Jesus. Finally, he became sick—so ill— that the doctors called him a "museum of tropical diseases." So he returned to England; his life seemingly near its end. But he was thankful for what God had used him to do in leading others to Jesus.

Then, while walking the streets one day after his return, he saw an announcement of a missionary rally to be held that evening. In large print, at the top, it said, "Cannibals Need Missionaries." He laughed at the wording, but went to the meeting that night.

There the conviction came to him that he must go as a missionary to Africa.

His friends thought he was beside himself. Aged, a grandfather, still a sick man,–and he was planning to go to Africa!

And to Africa Studd went, there to work in areas where no white man had ever been. He worked day and night to give the native people the gospel of what Jesus could do for their lives.

For seventeen pain-racked years he worked in Africa, without once going home on furlough. As he worked, he trained others to work with him. He had given everything for Christ, and others came to share in his sacrifice and in his labors.

Finally, he was in so much pain that his personal attendant, Jimmy Taylor, thought that Studd was definitely dying. Getting up at 11 p.m., he went over to give him a pain-killing injection so that he could get some sleep.

Later, at 3:00 p.m., Taylor became concerned and thought he had better check to see that C.T. Studd was still alive. Arriving at his hut, he found it empty! On the table were several pages with writing on them, and a brief note. It read: "Dear Jim, I have translated a couple more chapters of Acts and I am off now on my bicycle to reach another tribe for Jesus."

This was just 4 hours after Taylor had helped him so that he could have one "last" night of rest before the end. Even though many people would feel they had a right to retire after so many years of work—especially when compassed with pain or sickness—not so with Studd. On he went, for several more years.

A young man named Harrison, hearing of the work of C.T. Studd in Africa, determined to help him. Upon his arrival, he thought that he would immediately begin preaching. But, Studd, learning of his abilities in carpentry and shoe repairing, set him to work for a time using those much-needed skills.

Now, Harrison could have done that back in England and made good money at it. But he was glad to do whatever he was asked, for he knew that he was doing it for Jesus.

With such an attitude, he was eventually placed in charge of many things at the mission station, and when Studd died, Harrison became his successor.

To live with Jesus is to work with Jesus.

God is the source of life and light and joy to the universe. Like rays of light from the sun, like the streams of water bursting from a living spring, blessings flow out from Him to all His creatures. And wherever the life of God is in the hearts of men, it will flow out to others in love and blessing.

Our Saviour's joy was in the uplifting and redemption of fallen men. For this He counted not His life dear unto Himself, but endured the cross, despising the shame. So angels are ever engaged in working for the happiness of others. This is their joy. That which selfish hearts would regard as humiliating service, ministering to those who are wretched and in every way inferior in character and rank is the work of sinless angels. The spirit of Christ's self-sacrificing love is the spirit that pervades heaven and is the very essence of its bliss. This is the spirit that Christ's followers will possess, the work that they will do.

When the love of Christ is enshrined in the heart, like sweet fragrance it cannot be hidden. Its holy influence will be felt by all with whom we come in contact. The spirit of Christ in the heart is like a spring in the desert, flowing to refresh all and making those who are ready to perish eager to drink of the water of life.

Love to Jesus will be manifested in a desire to work as He worked for the blessing and uplifting of humanity. It will lead to love, tenderness, and sympathy toward all the creatures of our heavenly Father's care.

The Saviour's life on earth was not a life of ease and devotion to Himself, but He toiled with persistent, earnest, untiring effort for the salvation of lost mankind. From the manger to Calvary He followed the path of self-denial and sought not to be released from arduous tasks, painful travels, and exhausting care and labor. He said, "The Son of man came not to be ministered unto, but to minister, and to give His life a ransom for many." *Matthew 20:28*. This was the one great object of His life. Everything else was secondary and subservient. It was His meat and drink to do the will of God and to finish His work. Self and self-interest had no part in His labor.

Ready to Share in the Sacrifice

So those who are the partakers of the grace of Christ will be ready to make any sacrifice, that others for whom He died may share the heavenly gift. They will do all they can to make the world better for their stay in it. This spirit is the sure outgrowth of a soul truly converted. No sooner does one come to Christ than there is born in his heart a desire to make known to others what a precious friend he has found in Jesus; the saving and sanctifying truth cannot be shut up in his heart. If we are clothed with the righteousness of Christ and are filled with the joy of His indwelling Spirit, we shall not be able to hold our peace. If we have tasted and seen that the Lord is good we shall have something to tell. Like Philip when he found the Saviour, we shall invite others into His presence. We shall seek to present to them the attractions of Christ and the unseen realities of the world to come. There will be an intensity of desire to follow in the path that Jesus trod. There will be an earnest longing that those around us may "behold the Lamb of God, which taketh away the sin of the world" (*John 1:29*).

And the effort to bless others will react in blessings upon ourselves. This was the purpose of God in giving us a part to act in the plan of redemption. He has granted men the privilege of becoming partakers of the divine nature and, in their turn, of diffusing blessings to their fellow men. This is the highest honor, the greatest joy, that it is possible for God to bestow upon men. Those who thus become participants in labors of love are brought nearest to their Creator.

God might have committed the message of the gospel and all the work of loving ministry to the heavenly angels. He might have employed other means for accomplishing His purpose. But, in His infinite love, He chose to make us co-workers with Himself, with Christ and the angels, that we might share the blessing, the joy, the spiritual uplifting, which results from this unselfish ministry.

We are brought into sympathy with Christ through the fellowship of His sufferings. Every act of self-sacrifice for the good of others strengthens the spirit of beneficence in the giver's heart, allying him more closely to the Redeemer of the world, who "was rich, yet for your sakes . . became poor, that ye through His poverty might be rich" (2 *Corinthians 8:9*). And it is only as we thus fulfill the divine purpose in our creation that life can be a blessing to us.

Working Leads to Growing

If you will go to work as Christ designs that His disciples shall, and win souls for Him, you will feel the need of a deeper experience and a greater knowledge in divine things, and will hunger and thirst after righteousness. You will plead with God, and your faith will be strengthened, and your soul will drink deeper drafts at the well of salvation. Encountering opposition and trials will drive you to the Bible and prayer. You will grow in grace and the knowledge of Christ, and will develop a rich experience.

The spirit of unselfish labor for others gives depth, stability, and Christlike loveliness to the character, and brings peace and happiness to its possessor. The aspirations are elevated. There is no room for sloth or selfishness. Those who thus exercise the Christian graces will grow and will become strong to work for God. They will have clear spiritual perceptions, a steady, growing faith, and an increased power in prayer. The Spirit of God, moving upon their spirit, calls forth the sacred harmonies of the soul in answer to the divine touch. Those who thus devote themselves to unselfish effort for the good of others are most surely working out their own salvation.

The Only Way to Grow

The only way to grow in grace is to be disinterestedly doing the very work which Christ has enjoined upon us—to engage, to the extent of our ability, in helping and blessing those who need the help we can give them. Strength comes by exercise; activity is the very condition of life. Those who endeavor to maintain Christian life by passively accepting the blessings that come through the means of grace, and doing nothing for Christ, are simply trying to live by eating without working. And, in the spiritual as in the natural world, this always results in degeneration and decay. A man who would refuse to exercise his limbs would soon lose all power to use them. Thus the Christian who will not exercise his God-given powers not only fails to grow up into Christ, but he loses the strength that he already had.

The church of Christ is God's appointed agency for the salvation of men. Its mission is to carry the gospel to the world. And the obligation rests upon all Christians. Everyone, to the extent of his talent and opportunity, is to fulfill the Saviour's commission. The love of Christ, revealed to us, makes us debtors to all who know Him not. God has given us light, not for ourselves alone, but to shed upon them.

If the followers of Christ were awake to duty, there would be thousands where there is one today proclaiming the gospel in heathen lands. And all who could not personally engage in the work would yet sustain it with their means, their sympathy, and their prayers. And there would be far more earnest labor for souls in Christian countries.

We need not go to heathen lands, or even leave the narrow circle of the home, if it is there that our duty lies, in order to work for Christ. We can do this in the home circle, in the church, among those with whom we associate, and with whom we do business.

The greater part of our Saviour's life on earth was spent in patient toil in the carpenter's shop at Nazareth. Ministering angels attended the Lord of life as He walked side by side with peasants and laborers, unrecognized and unhonored. He was as faithfully fulfilling His mission while working at His humble trade as when He healed the sick or walked upon the storm-tossed waves of Galilee. So in the humblest duties and lowliest positions of life, we may walk and work with Jesus.

Begin Right Where You Are

The apostle says, "Let every man, wherein he is called, therein abide with God." *1 Corinthians 7:24*. The businessman may conduct his business in a way that will glorify his Master because of his fidelity. If he is a true follower of Christ, he will carry his religion into everything that is done and reveal to men the spirit of Christ. The mechanic may be a diligent and faithful representative of Him who toiled in the lowly walks of life among the hills of Galilee. Everyone who names the name of Christ should so work that others, by seeing his good works, may be led to glorify their Creator and Redeemer.

Many have excused themselves from rendering their gifts to the service of Christ because others were possessed of superior endowments and advantages. The opinion has prevailed that only those who are especially talented are required to consecrate their abilities to the service of God. It has come to be understood by many that talents are given to only a certain favored class to the exclusion of others who of course are not called upon to share in the toils or the rewards. But it is not so represented in the parable. When the master of the house called his servants, he gave to every man his work.

With a loving spirit we may perform life's humblest duties "as to the Lord" (*Colossians 3:23*). If the love of God is in the heart, it will be manifested in the life. The sweet savor of Christ will surround us, and our influence will elevate and bless.

You are not to wait for great occasions or to expect extraordinary abilities before you go to work for God. You need not have a thought of what the world will think of you. If your daily life is a testimony to the purity and sincerity of your faith, and others are convinced that you desire to benefit them, your efforts will not be wholly lost.

The humblest and poorest of the disciples of Jesus can be a blessing to others. They may not realize that they are doing any special good, but by their unconscious influence they may start waves of blessing that will widen and deepen, and the blessed results they may never know until the day of final reward. They do not feel or know that they are doing anything great. They are not required to weary themselves with anxiety about success. They have only to go forward quietly, doing faithfully the work that God's providence assigns, and their life will not be in vain. Their own souls will be growing more and more into the likeness of Christ; they are workers together with God in this life and are thus fitting for the higher work and the unshadowed joy of the life to come.

Giving thanks always for all things
Unto God and the Father
In the name of our Lord Jesus Christ.
— Ephesians 5:20

In everything by prayer and supplication
With thanksgiving
Let your requests be made known
Unto God.
— Philippians 4:6

O magnify the Lord with me,
And let us exalt His name together.
— Psalm 34:3

Sanctify them through Thy truth:
Thy Word is truth. –John 17:17

For whatsoever things were written aforetime
Were written for our learning,
That we through patience
And comfort of the Scriptures
Might have hope.
— Romans 15:4

These are written, that ye might believe
That Jesus is the Christ, the Son of God;
And that believing,
ye might have life through His name.
— John 20:31

If any of you lack wisdom,
Let him ask of God,
That giveth to all men liberally.
– James 1:5-6

CHAPTER TEN

Learning of Him

A man who would rather have his family haul water from a nearby polluted well—instead of going to a clean spring farther off—was shown, through a microscope, the germs in the well water.

Not liking the looks of the germs wriggling in the water, he took a large stick and broke the microscope . . and continued to drink the well water.

An unknown native, dressed in skins and leading a goat, came to the home of a woman missionary in Africa. Striking his spear into the ground, he said, "White lady, has God's Book arrived in our country?"

"Are you interested in God's Book?" she asked.

"Yes, my son brought me these pieces of paper, and has been teaching me the words, 'God so loved the world, that He gave His only begotten Son.' I heard that God's Book had arrived, and I have walked for five days, and I have brought this goat to buy God's Book."

Bringing him a Bible, she showed him where the memorized words were printed.

"Give me that Book," he pled, "and you may keep this goat." Then, walking back and forth, he pressed the Book to his heart, and said: "God's Book. God's Book! He has spoken to us in our own language!"

Dr. A.G. Congdon was honest with himself. In despair at the situation, he went to R.A. Torrey in Baraboo, Wisconsin, and told him of his problem.

"I am a complete failure as a preacher and Bible teacher. I have become as dry as dust, and the Bible is dry as dust to me. I must return to my first love for God's Word or leave the ministry. Please tell me how to study it so it will mean something to me."

Dr. Torrey replied, "Read it." "But I do read it." "Read it some more." Congdon replied, "How?"

Torrey said, "Take some book of the Bible and read it twelve times a day for a month."

"What book could I read that many hours a day, working as many hours as I do?"

He replied, "Try Second Peter."

Dr. Congdon tells what happened as a result:

"I did just what he said. My wife and I read Second Peter three or four times in the morning, two or three times at noon, and two or three times at dinner. Soon I was talking Second Peter to everyone I met.

"It seemed as though the stars in the heavens were singing the story of Second Peter. I read Second Peter on my knees, marking passages.

Teardrops mingled with the penciled colors, and I told my wife, 'See how I have ruined this part of my Bible.'

"'Yes,' she said, 'but as the pages have been getting darker, your life has been getting whiter.'"

And that is the power of the Bible. It is your pathway to a knowledge of God—and to a changed life.

As you read it earnestly, prayerfully, the Holy Spirit will guide you in its study.

But do more than read: also share it with others. Where should you begin? R.A. Torrey's advice is excellent. Others have tried it with equal success.

And consider going deeply into a longer book. The Gospel of John is a doorway to heaven; the Book of Ephesians is inside heaven. Read that book for a month and you will be a changed person.

In this chapter are more ways to study the Bible.

Many are the ways in which God is seeking to make Himself known to us and bring us into communion with Him. Nature speaks to our senses without ceasing. The open heart will be impressed with the love and glory of God as revealed through the works of His hands. The listening ear can hear and understand the communications of God through the things of nature. The green fields, the lofty trees, the buds and flowers, the passing cloud, the falling rain, the babbling brook, the glories of the heavens, speak to our hearts, and invite us to become acquainted with Him who made them all.

Our Saviour bound up His precious lessons with the things of nature. The trees, the birds, the flowers of the valleys, the hills, the lakes, and the beautiful heavens, as well as the incidents and surroundings of daily life, were all linked with the words of truth, that His lessons might thus be often recalled to mind, even amid the busy cares of man's life of toil.

God would have His children appreciate His works and delight in the simple, quiet beauty with which He has adorned our earthly home. He is a lover of the beautiful. And above all that is outwardly attractive, He loves beauty of character; He would have us cultivate purity and simplicity, the quiet graces of the flowers.

If we will but listen, God's created works will teach us precious lessons of obedience and trust. From the stars that in their trackless courses through space follow from age to age their appointed path, down to the minutest atom, the things of nature obey the Creator's will. And God cares for everything and sustains everything that He has created. He who upholds the unnumbered worlds throughout immensity, at the same time cares for the wants of the little brown sparrow that sings its humble song without fear. When men go forth to their daily toil, as when they engage in prayer; when they lie down at night, and when they rise in the morning; when the rich man feasts in his palace or when the poor man gathers his children about the scanty board, each is tenderly watched by the heavenly Father. No tears are shed that God does not notice. There is no smile that He does not mark.

If We Would but Believe

If we would but fully believe this, all undue anxieties would be dismissed. Our lives would not be so filled with disappointment as now; for everything, whether great or small, would be left in the hands of God, who is not perplexed by the multiplicity of cares or overwhelmed by their weight. We should then enjoy a rest of soul to which many have long been strangers.

As your senses delight in the attractive loveliness of the earth, think of the world that is to come, that shall never know the blight of sin and death; where the face of nature will no more wear the shadow of the curse. Let your imagination picture the home of the saved, and remember that it will be more glorious than your brightest imagination can portray. In the varied gifts of God in nature we see but the faintest gleaming of His glory. It is written, "Eye hath not seen, nor ear heard, neither have entered into the heart of man, the things which God hath prepared for them that love Him." *1 Corinthians 2:9.*

The poet and the naturalist have many things to say about nature, but it is the Christian who enjoys the beauty of the earth with the highest appreciation, because he recognizes his Father's handiwork and perceives His love in flower and shrub and tree. No one can fully appreciate the significance of hill and vale, river and sea, who does not look upon them as an expression of God's love to man.

The Bible, Our Lesson Book

God speaks to us through His providential workings and through the influence of His Spirit upon the heart. In our circumstances and surroundings, in the changes daily taking place around us, we may find precious lessons if our hearts are but open to discern them. The psalmist, tracing the work of God's providence, says, "The earth is full of the goodness of the Lord." *Psalm 33:5.* "Whoso is wise, and will observe these things, even they shall understand the loving-kindness of the Lord." *Psalm 107:43.*

God speaks to us in His Word. Here we have in clearer

lines the revelation of His character, of His dealings with men, and the great work of redemption. Here is open before us the history of patriarchs and prophets and other holy men of old. They were men "subject to like passions as we are" (*James 5:17*). We see how they struggled through discouragements like our own, how they fell under temptation as we have done, and yet took heart again and conquered through the grace of God; and, beholding, we are encouraged in our striving after righteousness. As we read of the precious experiences granted them, of the light and love and blessing it was theirs to enjoy, and of the work they wrought through the grace given them, the spirit that inspired them kindles a flame of holy emulation in our hearts and a desire to be like them in character—like them to walk with God.

Jesus said of the Old Testament Scriptures,—and how much more is it true of the New,—"They are they which testify of Me" (*John 5:39*), the Redeemer, Him in whom our hopes of eternal life are centered. Yes, the whole Bible tells of Christ. From the first record of creation—for "without Him was not anything made that was made" (*John 1:3*)—to the closing promise, "Behold, I come quickly" (*Revelation 22:12*), we are reading of His works and listening to His voice. If you would become acquainted with the Saviour, study the Holy Scriptures.

Fill the whole heart with the words of God. They are the living water, quenching your burning thirst. They are the living bread from heaven. Jesus declares, "Except ye eat the flesh of the Son of man, and drink His blood, ye have no life in you." And He explains Himself by saying, "The words that I speak unto you, they are spirit, and they are life." *John 6:53, 63*. Our bodies are built up from what we eat and drink; and as in the natural economy, so in the spiritual economy: It is what we meditate upon that will give tone and strength to our spiritual nature.

Our Study throughout Eternity

The theme of redemption is one that the angels desire to look into; it will be the science and the song of the redeemed throughout the ceaseless ages of eternity. Is it not worthy of careful thought and study now? The infinite mercy and love of Jesus, the sacrifice made in our behalf, call for the most serious and solemn reflection. We should dwell upon the character of our dear Redeemer and Intercessor. We should meditate upon the mission of Him who came to save His people from their sins. As we thus contemplate heavenly themes, our faith and love will grow stronger, and our prayers will be more and more acceptable to God, because they will be more and more mixed with faith and love. They will be intelligent and fervent. There will be more constant confidence in Jesus and a daily, living experience in His power to save to the uttermost all that come unto God by Him.

As we meditate upon the perfections of the Saviour, we shall desire to be wholly transformed and renewed in the image of His purity. There will be a hungering and thirsting of soul to become like Him whom we adore. The more our thoughts are upon Christ, the more we shall speak of Him to others and represent Him to the world.

The Bible was not written for the scholar alone; on the contrary, it was designed for the common people. The great truths necessary for salvation are made as clear as noonday; and none will mistake and lose their way except those who follow their own judgment instead of the plainly revealed will of God.

We should not take the testimony of any man as to what the Scriptures teach, but should study the words of God for ourselves. If we allow others to do our thinking, we shall have crippled energies and contracted abilities. The noble powers of the mind may be so dwarfed by lack of exercise on themes worthy of their concentration as to lose their ability to grasp the deep meaning of the Word of God. The mind will enlarge if it is employed in tracing out the relation of the subjects of the Bible, comparing Scripture with Scripture and spiritual things with spiritual.

The Ennobling Power of Scripture

There is nothing more calculated to strengthen the intellect than the study of the Scriptures. No other book is so potent to elevate the thoughts, to give vigor to the faculties, as the broad, ennobling truths of the Bible. If God's Word were studied as it should be, men would have a breadth of mind, a nobility of character, and a stability of purpose rarely seen in these times.

But there is but little benefit derived from a hasty reading of the Scriptures. One may read the whole Bible through and yet fail to see its beauty or comprehend its deep and hidden meaning. One passage studied until its significance is clear to the mind and its relation to the plan of salvation is of more value than the perusal of many chapters with no definite purpose in view and no positive instruction gained. Keep your Bible with you. As you have opportunity, read it; fix the texts in your memory. Even while you are walking the streets you may read a passage and meditate upon it, thus fixing it in the mind.

We cannot obtain wisdom without earnest attention and prayerful study. Some portions of Scripture are indeed too plain to be misunderstood, but there are others whose meaning does not lie on the surface to be seen at a glance. Scripture must be compared with Scripture. There must be careful research and prayerful reflection. And such study will be richly repaid. As the miner discovers veins of precious metal concealed beneath the surface of the earth, so will he who perseveringly searches the Word of God as for hid treasure find truths of the greatest value, which are concealed from the view of the careless seeker. The words of inspiration, pondered in the heart, will be as streams flowing from the fountain of life.

Always Study it with Prayer

Never should the Bible be studied without prayer. Before opening its pages we should ask for the enlightenment of the Holy Spirit, and it will be given. When Nathanael came to Jesus, the Saviour exclaimed, "Behold an Israelite indeed, in whom is no guile!" Nathanael said, "Whence knowest Thou me?" Jesus answered, "Before that Philip called thee, when thou wast under the fig tree, I saw thee" (*John 1:47-48*). And Jesus will see us also in the secret places of prayer if we will seek Him for light that we may know what is truth.

Angels from the world of light will be with those who in humility of heart seek for divine guidance.

The Holy Spirit exalts and glorifies the Saviour. It is His office to present Christ, the purity of His righteousness, and the great salvation that we have through Him. Jesus says, "He shall receive of Mine, and shall show it unto you." *John 16:14*. The Spirit of truth is the only effectual teacher of divine truth. How must God esteem the human race, since He gave His Son to die for them and appoints His Spirit to be man's teacher and continual guide!

All Scripture is given by inspiration of God,
And is profitable for doctrine,
For reproof, for correction,
For instruction in righteousness,
That the man of God may be perfect,
Throughly furnished unto all good works.
— 2 Timothy 3:16-17

For the prophecy came not
In old time by the will of man;
But holy men of God spake
As they were moved
By the Holy Ghost.
— 2 Peter 1:21

To the law and to the testimony:
If they speak not according to this Word,
It is because there is no light in them.
— Isaiah 8:20

Blessed are they that hear the Word of God,
And keep it.
— Luke 11:28

Thy Word is a lamp unto my feet,
And a light unto my path.
–Psalm 119:105

CHAPTER ELEVEN

Praying to Him

How much does a prayer weigh? The only man I ever knew who tried to weigh one still doesn't know.

He owned a little grocery store on the west side.

The First World War had just ended, and it was the week before Christmas. A tired-looking woman came into the store and asked him for enough food to make up a Christmas dinner for her children. The grocer asked her how much she could afford to spend.

"My husband was killed in the war," she said, "and I have nothing to offer but a little prayer."

This grocer confesses that he was not very sentimental in those days. A grocery store could not be run like a bread line.

So he said, "Write it on paper," and turned about his business.

To his surprise, the woman plucked a piece of paper out of her bosom and handed it to him over the counter and said, "I did that during the night—watching over my sick baby."

The grocer took the paper before he could recover his surprise, and then regretted having done so! For what would he do with it; what could he say?

Then an idea suddenly came to him. He placed the paper, without even reading the prayer upon it, on the weight side of his old-fashioned scales. Picking up a loaf of bread from nearby, he said, "We shall see how much this food is worth."

To his astonishment, the scale would not go down when he laid the loaf on the other side. To his confusion and embarrassment, it would not go down—though he kept on adding more food, anything he could lay his hands on quickly—for people were watching him.

He tried to be gruff, and he was making a bad job of it. His face got red, and he felt flustered. So finally he said, "Well, that's all the scales will hold anyway. Here's a bag. You'll have to put it in yourself. I'm busy."

With what sounded like a gasp or a little sob, she took the bag and started packing in the food, wiping her eyes on her sleeves every time her arm was free to do so. He tried not to look, but he could not help seeing that he had given her a pretty big bag and that it was not full when she had finished. So, without saying anything, he tossed down the counter to her several expensive items. Trying not to notice, he saw a timid smile of grateful understanding glistening in her eyes.

When the woman was gone, he went to look at the scales, scratching his head and shaking the scales in puzzlement. Then he found the solution. When the paper had been placed on it, the scales had broken.

That grocer is an old man now. His hair is white. But he has never forgotten the incident. He never saw the woman again. And, come to think of it, he had never seen her before. Yet for the rest of his life, he remembered her better than any other customer he ever had.

And he knew it had not been just his imagination, for he still had the slip of paper upon which the woman's prayer had been written: "Please, Lord, give us this day our daily bread."

In this chapter, you will learn about prayer,—that wonderful gateway to the throne of God. For this is what you want to know: how to pray.

Through nature and revelation, through His providence, and by the influence of His Spirit, God speaks to us. But these are not enough; we need also to pour out our hearts to Him. In order to have spiritual life and energy, we must have actual intercourse with our heavenly Father. Our minds may be drawn out toward Him; we may meditate upon His works, His mercies, His blessings; but this is not, in the fullest sense, communing with Him. In order to commune with God, we must have something to say to Him concerning our actual life.

Prayer is the opening of the heart to God as to a friend. Not that it is necessary in order to make known to God what we are, but in order to enable us to receive Him. Prayer does not bring God down to us, but brings us up to Him.

When Jesus was upon the earth, He taught His disciples how to pray. He directed them to present their daily needs before God, and to cast all their care upon Him. And the assurance He gave them, that their petitions should be heard, is assurance also to us.

Jesus Himself, while He dwelt among men, was often in prayer. Our Saviour identified Himself with our needs and weakness, in that He became a suppliant, a petitioner, seeking from His Father fresh supplies of strength, that He might come forth braced for duty and trial. He is our example in all things. He is a brother in our infirmities, "in all points tempted like as we are"; but as the sinless one His nature recoiled from evil; He endured struggles and torture of soul in a world of sin. His humanity made prayer a necessity and a privilege. He found comfort and joy in communion with His Father. And if the Saviour of men, the Son of God, felt the need of prayer, how much more should feeble, sinful mortals feel the necessity of fervent, constant prayer.

Our heavenly Father waits to bestow upon us the fullness of His blessing. It is our privilege to drink largely at the fountain of boundless love. What a wonder it is that we pray so little! God is ready and willing to hear the sincere prayer of the humblest of His children, and yet there is much manifest reluctance on our part to make known our wants to God.

What can the angels of heaven think of poor helpless human beings, who are subject to temptation, when God's heart of infinite love yearns toward them, ready to give them more than they can ask or think, and yet they pray so little and have so little faith? The angels love to bow before God; they love to be near Him. They regard communion with God as their highest joy; and yet the children of earth, who need so much the help that God only can give, seem satisfied to walk without the light of His Spirit, the companionship of His presence.

Neglecting to Pray

The darkness of the evil one encloses those who neglect to pray. The whispered temptations of the enemy entice them to sin; and it is all because they do not make use of the privileges that God has given them in the divine appointment of prayer. Why should the sons and daughters of God be reluctant to pray, when prayer is the key in the hand of faith to unlock heaven's storehouse, where are treasured the boundless resources of Omnipotence? Without unceasing prayer and diligent watching we are in danger of growing careless and of deviating from the right path. The adversary seeks continually to obstruct the way to the mercy seat, that we may not by earnest supplication and faith obtain grace and power to resist temptation.

There are certain conditions upon which we may expect that God will hear and answer our prayers. One of the first of these is that we feel our need of help from Him. He has promised, "I will pour water upon him that is thirsty, and floods upon the dry ground." *Isaiah 44:3*. Those who hunger and thirst after righteousness, who long after God, may be sure that they will be filled. The heart must be open to the Spirit's influence, or God's blessing cannot be received.

Our Need Is the Guarantee

Our great need is itself an argument and pleads most eloquently in our behalf. But the Lord is to be sought unto to do these things for us. He says, "Ask, and it shall be given you." *Matthew 7:7*. And "He that spared not His own Son, but delivered Him up for us all, how shall He not with Him also freely give us all things?" *Romans 8:32*.

If we regard iniquity in our hearts, if we cling to any known sin, the Lord will not hear us; but the prayer of the penitent, contrite soul is always accepted. When all known wrongs are righted, we may believe that God will answer our petitions. Our own merit will never commend us to the favor of God; it is the worthiness of Jesus that will save us, His blood that will cleanse us; yet we have a work to do in complying with the conditions of acceptance.

Another element of prevailing prayer is faith. "He that cometh to God must believe that He is, and that He is a rewarder of them that diligently seek Him." *Hebrews 11:6*. Jesus said to His disciples, "What things soever ye desire, when ye pray, believe that ye receive them, and ye shall have them." *Mark 11:24*. Do we take Him at His word?

The assurance is broad and unlimited, and He is faithful who has promised. When we do not receive the very things we asked for, at the time we ask, we are still to believe that the Lord hears and that He will answer our prayers. We are so erring and short-sighted that we sometimes ask for things that would not be a blessing to us; and our heavenly Father in love answers our prayers by giving us that which will be for our highest good—that which we ourselves would desire if, with vision divinely enlightened, we could see all things as they really are. When our prayers seem not to be answered, we are to cling to the promise; for the time of answering will surely come, and we shall receive the blessing we need most. But to claim that prayer will always be answered in the very way and for the particular thing that we desire is presumption. God is too wise to err and too good to withhold any good thing from them that walk uprightly. Then do not fear to trust Him, even though you do not see the immediate answer to your prayers. Rely upon His sure promise, "Ask, and it shall be given you" (*Matthew 7:7*).

Come in All Your Helplessness to God

If we take counsel with our doubts and fears, or try to solve everything that we cannot see clearly, before we have faith, perplexities will only increase and deepen. But if we come to God, feeling helpless and dependent, as we really are, and in humble, trusting faith make known our wants to Him whose knowledge is infinite, who sees everything in creation, and who governs everything by His will and word, He can and will attend to our cry, and will let light shine into our hearts. Through sincere prayer we are brought into connection with the mind of the Infinite. We may have no remarkable evidence at the time that the face of our Redeemer is bending over us in compassion and love, but this is even so. We may not feel His visible touch, but His hand is upon us in love and pitying tenderness.

When we come to ask mercy and blessing from God we should have a spirit of love and forgiveness in our own hearts. How can we pray, "Forgive us our debts, as we forgive our debtors" (*Matthew 6:12*), and yet indulge an unforgiving spirit? If we expect our own prayers to be heard we must forgive others in the same manner and to the same extent as we hope to be forgiven.

Perseverance in prayer has been made a condition of receiving. We must pray always if we would grow in faith and experience. We are to be "instant in prayer" (*Romans 12:12*), to "continue in prayer, and watch in the same with thanksgiving" (*Colossians 4:2*). Peter exhorts believers to be "sober, and watch unto prayer" *(1 Peter 4:7)*. Paul directs, "In everything by prayer and supplication with thanksgiving let your requests be made known unto God." *Philippians 4:6*. "But ye, beloved," says Jude, "praying in the Holy Ghost, keep yourselves in the love of God" (*Jude 20-21*). Unceasing prayer is the unbroken union of the soul with God, so that life from God flows into our life; and from our life, purity and holiness flow back to God.

There is necessity for diligence in prayer; let nothing hinder you. Make every effort to keep open the communion between Jesus and your own soul. Seek every opportunity to go where prayer is wont to be made. Those who are really seeking for communion with God will be seen in the prayer meeting, faithful to do their duty and earnest and anxious to reap all the benefits they can gain. They will improve every opportunity of placing themselves where they can receive the rays of light from heaven.

Praying Alone with God

We should pray in the family circle. And, above all, we must not neglect secret prayer; for this is the life of the soul. It is impossible for the soul to flourish while prayer is neglected. Family or public prayer alone is not sufficient. In solitude let the soul be laid open to the inspecting eye of God. Secret prayer is to be heard only by the prayer-hearing God. No curious ear is to receive the burden of such petitions. In secret prayer the soul is free from surrounding influences, free from excitement. Calmly, yet fervently, will it reach out after God. Sweet and abiding will be the influence emanating from Him who seeth in secret, whose ear is open to hear the prayer arising from the heart. By calm, simple faith the soul holds communion with God and gathers to itself rays of divine light to strengthen and sustain it in the conflict with Satan. God is our tower of strength.

Pray in your closet; and, as you go about your daily labor, let your heart be often uplifted to God. It was thus that Enoch walked with God. These silent prayers rise like precious incense before the throne of grace. Satan cannot overcome him whose heart is thus stayed upon God.

Pray Everywhere

There is no time or place in which it is inappropriate to offer up a petition to God. There is nothing that can prevent us from lifting up our hearts in the spirit of earnest prayer. In the crowds of the street, in the midst of a business engagement, we may send up a petition to God and plead for divine guidance, as did Nehemiah when he made his request before King Artaxerxes. A closet of communion may be found wherever we are. We should have the door of the heart open continually and our invitation going up that Jesus may come and abide as a heavenly guest in the soul.

Although there may be a tainted, corrupted atmosphere around us, we need not breathe its miasma, but may live in the pure air of heaven. We may close every door to impure imaginings and unholy thoughts by lifting the soul into the presence of God through sincere prayer. Those whose hearts are open to receive the support and blessing of God will walk in a holier atmosphere than that of earth and will have constant communion with heaven.

We need to have more distinct views of Jesus and a fuller comprehension of the value of eternal realities. The beauty of holiness is to fill the hearts of God's children; and that this may be accomplished, we should seek for divine disclosures of heavenly things.

Let the soul be drawn out and upward, that God may grant us a breath of the heavenly atmosphere. We may keep so near to God that, in every unexpected trial, our thoughts will turn to Him as naturally as the flower turns to the sun.

Continual Prayer

Keep your wants, your joys, your sorrows, your cares, and your fears before God. You cannot burden Him; you cannot weary Him. He who numbers the hairs of your head is not indifferent to the wants of His children. "The Lord is very pitiful, and of tender mercy." *James 5:11*. His heart of love is touched by our sorrows and even by our utterances of them. Take to Him everything that perplexes the mind. Nothing is too great for Him to bear, for He holds up worlds, He rules over all the affairs of the universe. Nothing that in any way concerns our peace is too small for Him to notice. There is no chapter in our experience too dark for Him to read; there is no perplexity too difficult for Him to unravel. No calamity can befall the least of His children, no anxiety harass the soul, no joy cheer, no sincere prayer escape the lips, of which our heavenly Father is unobservant, or in which He takes no immediate interest. "He healeth the broken in heart, and bindeth up their wounds." *Psalm 147:3*. The relation between God and each soul is as distinct and full as though there were not another soul upon the earth to share His watchcare, not another soul for whom He gave His beloved Son.

Jesus said, "Ye shall ask in My name: and I say not unto you, that I will pray the Father for you: for the Father Himself loveth you." *John 16:26-27*. "I have chosen you: . . that whatsoever ye shall ask of the Father in My name, He may give it you." *John 15:16*. But to pray in the name of Jesus is something more than a mere mention of that name at the beginning and the ending of a prayer. It is to pray in the mind and spirit of Jesus while we believe His promises, rely upon His grace, and work His works.

God does not mean that any of us should become hermits or monks and retire from the world in order to devote ourselves to acts of worship. The life must be like Christ's life—between the mountain and the multitude. He who does nothing but pray will soon cease to pray, or his prayers will become a formal routine. When men take themselves out of social life, away from the sphere of Christian duty and cross bearing, when they cease to work earnestly for the Master who worked earnestly for them, they lose the subject matter of prayer and have no incentive to devotion. Their prayers become personal and selfish. They cannot pray in regard to the wants of humanity or the upbuilding of Christ's kingdom, pleading for strength wherewith to work.

Praying Together

We sustain a loss when we neglect the privilege of associating together to strengthen and encourage one another in the service of God. The truths of His Word lose their vividness and importance in our minds. Our hearts cease to be enlightened and aroused by their sanctifying influence, and we decline in spirituality. In our association as Christians we lose much by lack of sympathy with one another. He who shuts himself up to himself is not filling the position that God designed he should. The proper cultivation of the social elements in our nature brings us into sympathy with others and is a means of development and strength to us in the service of God.

If Christians would associate together, speaking to each other of the love of God and of the precious truths of redemption, their own hearts would be refreshed and they would refresh one another. We may be daily learning more of our heavenly Father, gaining a fresh experience of His grace; then we shall desire to speak of His love; and as we do this, our own hearts will be warmed and encouraged. If we thought and talked more of Jesus, and less of self, we should have far more of His presence.

If we would but think of God as often as we have evidence of His care for us we should keep Him ever in our thoughts and should delight to talk of Him and to praise Him. We talk of temporal things because we have an interest in them. We talk of our friends because we love them; our joys and our sorrows are bound up with them. Yet we have infinitely greater reason to love God than to love our earthly friends; it should be the most natural thing in the world to make Him first in all our thoughts, to talk of His goodness, and tell of His power. The rich gifts He has bestowed upon us were not intended to absorb our thoughts and love so much that we should have nothing to give to God; they are constantly to remind us of Him and to bind us in bonds of love and gratitude to our heavenly Benefactor. We dwell too near the lowlands of earth. Let us raise our eyes to the open door of the Sanctuary above, where the light of the glory of God shines in the face of Christ, who "is able also to save them to the uttermost that come unto God by Him" (*Hebrews 7:25*).

Prayer that Is Praise

We need to praise God more "for His goodness, and for His wonderful works to the children of men!" *Psalm 107:8.* Our devotional exercises should not consist wholly in asking and receiving. Let us not be always thinking of our wants and never of the benefits we receive. We do not pray any too much, but we are too sparing of giving thanks. We are the constant recipients of God's mercies, and yet how little gratitude we express, how little we praise Him for what He has done for us.

Anciently the Lord bade Israel, when they met together for His service, "Ye shall eat before the Lord your God, and ye shall rejoice in all that ye put your hand unto, ye and your households, wherein the Lord thy God hath blessed thee" (*Deuteronomy 12:7*). That which is done for the glory of God should be done with cheerfulness, with songs of praise and thanksgiving, not with sadness and gloom.

Our God is a tender, merciful Father. His service should not be looked upon as a heart-saddening, distressing exercise. It should be a pleasure to worship the Lord and to take part in His work. God would not have His children, for whom so great salvation has been provided, act as if He were a hard, exacting taskmaster. He is their best friend; and, when they worship Him, He expects to be with them, to bless and comfort them, filling their hearts with joy and love. The Lord desires His children to take comfort in His service and to find more pleasure than hardship in His work. He desires that those who come to worship Him shall carry away with them precious thoughts of His care and love, that they may be cheered in all the employments of daily life, that they may have grace to deal honestly and faithfully in all things.

Our Deepest Thoughts and Feelings

We must gather about the cross. Christ and Him crucified should be the theme of contemplation, of conversation, and of our most joyful emotion. We should keep in our thoughts every blessing we receive from God; and, when we realize His great love, we should be willing to trust everything to the hand that was nailed to the cross for us.

The soul may ascend nearer heaven on the wings of praise. God is worshiped with song and music in the courts above, and as we express our gratitude, we are approximating to the worship of the heavenly hosts. "Whoso offereth praise glorifieth" God (*Psalm 50:23*). Let us with reverent joy come before our Creator, with "thanksgiving, and the voice of melody" (*Isaiah 51:3*).

O Thou that hearest prayer,
Unto Thee shall all flesh come.
— Psalm 65:2

He that cometh to God
Must believe that He is,
And that He is a rewarder
Of them that diligently seek Him.
— Hebrews 11:6

PROPHECIES ABOUT CHRIST

Read and believe: Predicted centuries before His birth, Jesus came and fulfilled hundreds of predictions. Here are a few of the prophecies. Yes, read and believe: Jesus is your Saviour, your Lord and your God. He is your hope for this life and for the life to come. *–vf*

THE SEED OF THE WOMAN–Gen 3:15; Gal 4:4; 1 Tim 2:15; Rev 12:5. BORN OF A VIRGIN–Psalms 22:10; 86:16; 116:16; Isa 7:14; 49:1; Jer 31:22: Micah 5:3; Matt 1:23; Luke 1:26-35. OF THE FAMILY OF SHEM–Gen 9:26. OF THE RACE OF THE HEBREWS–John 4:9; 18:35. OF THE SEED OF ABRAHAM–Gen 12:3; 18:18; 22:18; Matt 1:1; John 8:58; Acts 3:25; Heb 2:16. OF THE LINE OF ISAAC–Gen 17:19; 21:12; 26:4; Rom 9:7; Gal 4:23-28; Heb 11:18. OF JACOB (ISRAEL)–Gen 28:4-14; Ex 4:22; Num 24:7-17; Psalm 135:4, etc.; Isa 41:8; 49:6; Jer 14:8; Luke 1:68; 2:32; Acts 28:20. OF THE TRIBE OF JUDAH–Gen 49:10; 1 Chron 5:2; Micah 5:2; Matt 2:6; Heb 7:14; Rev 5:5. OF THE HOUSE OF DAVID–2 Sam 7:12-15; 1 Chron 17:11-14; 2 Chron 6:42; Psalms 89:4, 36; 132:10-17; Isa 9:7; 11:1; 55:3-4; Jer 23:5-6; Amos 9:11; Matt 1:1; Luke 1:69; 2:4; John 7:42; Acts 2:29-30; 13:23; Rom 1:3; 2 Tim 2:8; Rev 22:16. BORN AT BETHLEHEM, THE CITY OF DAVID–Micah 5:2; Matt 2:6; Luke 2:4; John 7:42. HIS SUFFERINGS–Gen 3:15; Psalms 22:1-18; 31:13; 89:38-45; Isa 53:1-12; Dan 9:26; Zech 13:6-7; Matt 26:31; Luke 24:26; John 1:29; 26:23. HIS DEATH ON THE CROSS–Num 21:9; Psalms 16:10; 22:16; 31:22; Isa 53:8-9; Dan 9:26; Matt 20:19; 26:2; John 3:14; 8:28; 12:32-33; 1 Cor 15:3; Col 2:14; Phil 2:8. HIS ENTOMBMENT AND EMBALMMENT–Isa 53:9; Matt 26:12; Mark 14:8; John 12:7; 19:40; 1 Cor 15:4. HIS RESURRECTION ON THE THIRD DAY–Psalms 16:10; 17:15; 49:15; 73:24; John 1:17; Matt 12:40; 16:4; 27:63; John 2:19; Acts 2:27-31; 13:35; 1 Cor 15:4. HIS ASCENSION INTO HEAVEN–Psalms 8:5-6; 47:5; 68:18; 110:1; Acts 1:9; 2:33; John 20:17; Eph 4:8-10; Heb 1:3; 2:9; Rev 12:5. HIS SECOND ADVENT–Isa 40:10; 62:11; Jer 23:5-6; Psalm 50:1-6; Job 19:25-29; Matt 24:3-30; 25:31-34; 26:64; John 5:25, 28-30; Acts 17:31; 24:25; Heb 9:28; Rev 14:14; 19:11-17.

— See page 109 for more.

CHAPTER TWELVE

Staying with Him

Dr. J.S. Bonnell, of New York City, received a telephone call from an army officer who had just arrived at Pennsylvania Station. He explained that he had only two days' leave before shipping out from the Pacific, but that he felt he must talk with Bonnell before seeing his family.

Putting aside his other plans, Dr. Bonnell told him to come to his office. Across the desk the officer explained that he could not go into battle in his present state of mind. He said he had lost his faith in the Bible and in God. Doubt seemed to overwhelm him. He had ceased to pray.

At this, Dr. Bonnell interrupted and said, "I am not interested in your doubts. There is no need spending your time or mine going in to them. Tell me about your sins."

A full moment of silence passed without a word. The silence was broken shortly after Dr. Bonnell asked the officer if he had pictures in his wallet of his family. The officer did.

The pictures were placed on the desk where both could see them—and then in a burst of tears the truth came out.

It is not our doubts that are the problem; it is our sins. It is not our questions that are the issue; it is our distance from God. When we come back to Him, confess our sins, and in His strength put them away,—then it is that our doubts dissolve, and our questions fade into nothingness. For when we have peace with Him, a new life can begin.

William T. Stidger tells of a young man who had been raised in a Christian home, but had wandered out into the world. He soon found it had nothing to offer but emptiness and dissatisfaction.

He could tell from his friends who had gone deeper than he into sin,—that the road ahead of him was only going to become more and more miserable.

One day, as he was walking the streets of a large city, he wished that there was someone who could help him. Seeing an old man sitting on a porch, he felt impressed to stop and talk with him. The elderly man was a Christian. As the two spoke together, the minutes turned into hours, and he showed the young man the road back to God.

In recalling it in later years, he said, All the stars had fallen out of my sky when I walked up to him; but one by one he put them all back again. For he told me that all I had to do to find God was to pray to Him—and give Him my sins—and my life—and cling to Him as His obedient child from then on.

Then there are those who have stepped very far out from the shadows of sins and doubt–into the bright sunlight of a deep walk by faith in God. One such man was George Muller of Bristol, England; he, trusting in God to provide, received and disbursed over $12 million, cared for 10,000 orphans, taught 122,000 students, distributed 282,000 Bibles and 1,500,000 Testaments, and erected five large orphan houses and supported many overseas missionaries—all by faith.

Learning of his experiences, a friend said to him one day: "You seem to live from hand to mouth!"

"Yes," said Mr. Muller, "it is our mouths, but God's hand."

Many, especially those who are young in the Christian life, are at times troubled with the suggestions of skepticism. There are in the Bible many things which they cannot explain, or even understand, and Satan employs these to shake their faith in the Scriptures as a revelation from God. They ask, "How shall I know the right way? If the Bible is indeed the Word of God, how can I be freed from these doubts and perplexities?"

God never asks us to believe, without giving sufficient evidence upon which to base our faith. His existence, His character, the truthfulness of His Word, are all established by testimony that appeals to our reason; and this testimony is abundant. Yet God has never removed the possibility of doubt. Our faith must rest upon evidence, not demonstration. Those who wish to doubt will have opportunity; while those who really desire to know the truth will find plenty of evidence on which to rest their faith.

It is impossible for finite minds fully to comprehend the character or the works of the Infinite One. To the keenest intellect, the most highly educated mind, that holy Being must ever remain clothed in mystery. "Canst thou by searching find out God? canst thou find out the Almighty unto perfection? It is as high as heaven; what canst thou do? deeper than hell; what canst thou know?" *Job 11:7-8.*

The apostle Paul exclaims, "O the depth of the riches both of the wisdom and knowledge of God! how unsearchable are His judgments, and His ways past finding out!" *Romans 11:33.* But though "clouds and darkness are round about Him . . righteousness and judgment are the foundation of His throne" (*Psalm 97:2, R.V.*). We can so far comprehend His dealings with us, and the motives by which He is actuated, that we may discern boundless love and mercy united to infinite power. We can understand as much of His purposes as it is for our good to know; and beyond this we must still trust the hand that is omnipotent, the heart that is full of love.

Mysteries in All Nature - and in God's Word

The Word of God, like the character of its divine Author, presents mysteries that can never be fully comprehended by finite beings. The entrance of sin into the world, the Incarnation of Christ, regeneration, the resurrection, and many other subjects presented in the Bible, are mysteries too deep for the human mind to explain or even fully comprehend. But we have no reason to doubt God's Word because we cannot understand the mysteries of His providence. In the natural world we are constantly surrounded with mysteries that we cannot fathom. The very humblest forms of life present a problem that the wisest of philosophers is powerless to explain. Everywhere are wonders beyond our ken. Should we then be surprised to find that in the spiritual world also there are mysteries that we cannot fathom? The difficulty lies solely in the weakness and narrowness of the human mind. God has given us in the Scriptures sufficient evidence of their divine character, and we are not to doubt His Word because we cannot understand all the mysteries of His providence.

The apostle Peter says that there are in Scripture "things hard to be understood, which they that are unlearned and unstable wrest . . unto their own destruction" (*2 Peter 3:16*). The difficulties of Scripture have been urged by skeptics as an argument against the Bible; but so far from this, they constitute a strong evidence of its divine inspiration. If it contained no account of God but that which we could easily comprehend; if His greatness and majesty could be grasped by finite minds, then the Bible would not bear the unmistakable credentials of divine authority. The very grandeur and mystery of the themes presented should inspire faith in it as the Word of God.

Simplicity - Yet the Greatest Truth

The Bible unfolds truth, with a simplicity and a perfect adaptation to the needs and longings of the human heart, that has astonished and charmed the most highly cultivated minds while it enables the humble and uncultured to discern the way of salvation. And yet these simply stated truths lay hold upon subjects so elevated, so far-reaching, so infinitely beyond the power of human comprehension, that we can accept them only because God has declared them. Thus the plan of redemption is laid open to us, so that every soul may see the steps he is to take in repentance toward God and faith toward our Lord Jesus Christ, in order to be saved in God's appointed way; yet beneath these truths, so easily understood, lie mysteries that are the hiding of His glory—mysteries that overpower the mind in its research, yet inspire the sincere seeker for truth with reverence and faith. The more he searches the Bible, the deeper is his conviction that it is the Word of the living God, and human reason bows before the majesty of divine revelation.

To acknowledge that we cannot fully comprehend the great truths of the Bible is only to admit that the finite mind is inadequate to grasp the infinite; that man, with his limited, human knowledge, cannot understand the purposes of Omniscience.

Because they cannot fathom all its mysteries, the skeptic and the infidel reject God's Word; and not all who profess to believe the Bible are free from danger on this point. The apostle says, "Take heed, brethren, lest there be in any of you an evil heart of unbelief, in departing from the living God." *Hebrews 3:12*. It is right to study closely the teachings of the Bible and to search into "the deep things of God" so far as they are revealed in Scripture (*1 Corinthians 2:10*). While "the secret things belong unto the Lord our God, . . those things which are revealed belong unto us." *Deuteronomy 29:29*. But it is Satan's work to pervert the investigative powers of the mind. A certain pride is mingled with the consideration of Bible truth, so that men feel impatient and defeated if they cannot explain every portion of Scripture to their satisfaction. It is too humiliating to them to acknowledge that they do not understand the inspired words. They are unwilling to wait patiently until God shall see fit to reveal the truth to them. They feel that their unaided human wisdom is sufficient to enable them to comprehend the Scripture; and, failing to do this, they virtually deny its authority. It is true that many theories and doctrines popularly supposed to be derived from the Bible have no foundation in its teaching, and indeed are contrary to the whole tenor of inspiration. These things have been a cause of doubt and perplexity to many minds. They are not, however, chargeable to God's Word, but to man's perversion of it.

Always Drawing Nearer

If it were possible for created beings to attain to a full understanding of God and His works, then, having reached this point, there would be for them no further discovery of truth, no growth in knowledge, no further development of mind or heart. God would no longer be supreme; and man, having reached the limit of knowledge and attainment, would cease to advance. Let us thank God that it is not so. God is infinite; in Him are "all the treasures of wisdom and knowledge" (*Colossians 2:3*). And through all eternity men may be ever searching, ever learning, and yet never exhaust the treasures of His wisdom, His goodness, and His power.

God intends that even in this life the truths of His Word shall be ever unfolding to His people. There is only one way in which this knowledge can be obtained. We can attain to an understanding of God's Word only through the illumination of that Spirit by which the word was given. "The things of God knoweth no man, but the Spirit of God"; "for the Spirit searcheth all things, yea, the deep things of God." *1 Corinthians 2:11, 10*. And the Saviour's promise to His followers was, "When He, the Spirit of truth, is come, He will guide you into all truth . . For He shall receive of Mine, and shall show it unto you." *John 16:13-14*.

The Faith of a Little Child

God desires man to exercise his reasoning powers; and the study of the Bible will strengthen and elevate the mind as no other study can. Yet we are to beware of deifying reason, which is subject to the weakness and infirmity of humanity. If we would not have the Scriptures clouded to our understanding, so that the plainest truths shall not be comprehended, we must have the simplicity and faith of a little child, ready to learn, and beseeching the aid of the Holy Spirit.

A sense of the power and wisdom of God, and of our inability to comprehend His greatness, should inspire us with humility; and we should open His Word, as we would enter His presence, with holy awe. When we come to the Bible, reason must acknowledge an authority superior to itself, and heart and intellect must bow to the great I AM.

There are many things apparently difficult or obscure, which God will make plain and simple to those who thus seek an understanding of them. But, without the guidance of the Holy Spirit, we shall be continually liable to wrest the Scriptures or to misinterpret them. There is much reading of the Bible that is without profit and in many cases a positive injury. When the Word of God is opened without reverence and without prayer; when the thoughts and affections are not fixed upon God, or in harmony with His will, the mind is clouded with doubts; and in the very study of the Bible, skepticism strengthens. The enemy takes control of the thoughts, and he suggests interpretations that are not correct. Whenever men are not in word and deed seeking to be in harmony with God, then, however learned they may be, they are liable to err in their understanding of Scripture, and it is not safe to trust to their explanations. Those who look to the Scriptures to find discrepancies, have not spiritual insight. With distorted vision they will see many causes for doubt and unbelief in things that are really plain and simple.

The Real Cause of Doubt

Disguise it as they may, the real cause of doubt and skepticism, in most cases, is the love of sin. The teachings and restrictions of God's Word are not welcome to the proud, sin-loving heart; and those who are unwilling to obey its requirements are ready to doubt its authority. In order to arrive at truth, we must have a sincere desire to know the truth and a willingness of heart to obey it. And all who come in this spirit to the study of the Bible will find abundant evidence that it is God's Word, and they may gain an understanding of its truths that will make them wise unto salvation.

Christ has said, "If any man willeth to do His will, he shall know of the teaching." *John 7:17, R.V.* Instead of questioning and caviling concerning that which you do not understand, give heed to the light that already shines upon you, and you will receive greater light. By the grace of Christ, perform every duty that has been made plain to your understanding, and you will be enabled to understand and perform those of which you are now in doubt.

There is an evidence that is open to all,—the most highly educated and the most illiterate,—the evidence of experience. God invites us to prove for ourselves the reality of His Word, the truth of His promises. He bids us "taste and see that the Lord is good" (*Psalm 34:8*). Instead of depending upon the word of another, we are to taste for ourselves. He declares, "Ask, and ye shall receive." *John 16:24*. His promises will be fulfilled. They have never failed; they never can fail. And as we draw near to Jesus, and rejoice in the fullness of His love, our doubt and darkness will disappear in the light of His presence.

The apostle Paul says that God "hath delivered us from the power of darkness, and hath translated us into the kingdom of His dear Son" (*Colossians 1:13*). And everyone who has passed from death unto life is able to "set to his seal that God is true" (*John 3:33*). He can testify, "I needed help, and I found it in Jesus. Every want was supplied, the hunger of my soul was satisfied; and now the Bible is to me the revelation of Jesus Christ. Do you ask why I believe in Jesus? Because He is to me a divine Saviour. Why do I believe the Bible? Because I have found it to be the voice of God to my soul." We may have the witness in ourselves that the Bible is true, that Christ is the Son of God. We know that we are not following cunningly devised fables.

Growing in Grace and Understanding

Peter exhorts his brethren to "grow in grace, and in the knowledge of our Lord and Saviour Jesus Christ" (*2 Peter 3:18*). When the people of God are growing in grace, they will be constantly obtaining a clearer understanding of His Word. They will discern new light and beauty in its sacred truths. This has been true in the history of the church in all ages, and thus it will continue to the end. "The path of the righteous is as the light of dawn, that shineth more and more unto the perfect day." *Proverbs 4:18, R.V., margin.*

By faith we may look to the hereafter and grasp the pledge of God for a growth of intellect, the human faculties uniting with the divine, and every power of the soul being brought into direct contact with the Source of light. We may rejoice that all which has perplexed us in the providences of God will then be made plain, things hard to be understood will then find an explanation; and where our finite minds discovered only confusion and broken purposes, we shall see the most perfect and beautiful harmony. "Now we see through a glass, darkly; but then face to face: now I know in part; but then shall I know even as also I am known." *1 Corinthians 13:12.*

But if we walk in the light,
As He is in the light,
We have fellowship one with another,
And the blood of Jesus Christ, His Son
Cleanseth us from all sin.
— I John 1:7

By faith Abraham,
When he was called . .
Obeyed.
— Hebrews 11:8

For we are made partakers of Christ,
If we hold the beginning of our confidence
Steadfast unto the end.
— Hebrews 3:14

Be thou faithful unto death
And I will give thee a crown of life.
— Revelation 2:10

Cast thy burden upon the Lord,
and He shall sustain thee.
– Psalm 55:22

PROPHECIES ABOUT CHRIST

THE SON OF GOD–2 Sam 7:14; 1 Chron 17:13; Psalms 2:7; 72:1; Prov 30:4; Dan 3:25; Mark 1:1; Luke 1:35; Matt 3:17; 17:5; John 1:34-50; 3:16-18; 20:31; Heb 1:1-5; Rom 1:4; 1 John 4:14-15; Rev 1:5-6. THE SON OF MAN–Psalm 8:4-5; Dan 7:13; John 1:51; 3:13; 5:17; Matt 16:13-16; 26:63; Heb 2:7; Rev 1:13; 14:14. THE HOLY ONE–Deut 33:8; Psalms 16:10; 89:19; Isa 10:17; 29:23; 49:7; Hos 11:9; Hab 1:12; 3:3; Mark 1:24; Luke 1:35; 4:34; 1 John 2:20. THE RIGHTEOUS ONE–Isaiah 41:2; Jer 23:5; Zech 9:9; Psalm 34:19, 21; Luke 1:17; Matt 27:19-24; Luke 23:47; Acts 3:14; 7:52; 22:14; 1 John 2:1, 29; James 5:6. THE WISDOM OF GOD–Prov 8:22-30; Matt 11:19; Luke 11:49; 1 Cor 1:24. THE WORD OF GOD–Gen 15:1-4; 1 Sam 3:1-21; 2 Sam 7:4, 1 Kings 17:8-24; Psalm 33:6; Isa 40:8; Jer 25:3; Micah 4:2; John 1:1-14; 3:34; Luke 1:2; Heb 4:12; 11:3; 1 Pet 1:23; 2 Pet 3:5; Rev 19:13. THE REDEEMER OR SAVIOUR–Gen 48:16; Job 19:25-27; Psalm 19:14; Isa 41:14; 44:6; 47:4; 59:20; 62:11; 63:1; Jer 50:34; Matt 1:21; Luke 2:11; John 1:29; Acts 5:31; Rom 11:26; Rev 5:9. THE LAMB OF GOD–Gen 22:8; Isa 53:7; John 1:29; Acts 8:32-35; 1 Pet 1:19; Rev 5:6; 13:8; 15:3; 21:22; 22:1. THE MEDIATOR, INTERCESSOR AND ADVOCATE–Job 33:23: Isa 53:12; 59:16; Luke 23:34; 1 Tim 2:5; Heb 9:15; 1 John 2:1; Rev 5:9. SHILOH, THE APOSTLE–Gen 49:10; Ex 4:13; Matt 15:24; Luke 4:18; John 9:7; 17:3; 20:21; Heb 3:1. THE HIGH PRIEST–Psalm 110:4; Isa 59:16; Heb 3:1; 4:14; 5:10; 9:11. THE PROPHET LIKE MOSES–Deut 18:15-19; Mark 6:15; Luke 24:19; John 1:17-21; 6:14; Acts 3:22-23. THE LEADER OR CHIEF CAPTAIN–Josh 5:14; 1 Chron 5:2; Isa 55:4; Micah 5:2; Dan 9:25; Matt 2:6; Heb 2:10. THE MESSIAH, CHRIST, KING OF ISRAEL–1 Sam 2:10; 2 Sam 7:12; Psalms 2:2, 6; 45:1, 6; 72:1; 89:38; Isa 61:1; Dan 9:26; Matt 2:2-4; 16:16; Luke 23:2; John 1:41-49; 6:69; Acts 4:26-27; 10:38. THE GOD OF ISRAEL–Ex 24:10-11; Judges 11:23; 1 Sam 5:11; 1 Chron 17:24; Psalm 41:13; Isa 45:3; Ezek 8:4; Matt 15:31; 22:37; John 20:38. KING OF KINGS, AND LORD OF LORDS–Psalms 89:27; 110:1; Dan 7:13-14; Matt 28:18; John 3:35; 13:3; 1 Cor 15:25; Eph 1:20-22; Col 3:1; Rev 19:16.

CHAPTER THIRTEEN

Rejoicing in Him

For many years Eva Tavor had been unable to see. Doctors offered no hope. All the brightness of life seemed blotted out, but in the darkness she learned to love and trust in a Saviour that she had so often ignored when she earlier had sight.

She found the verse that says, "Yea, the darkness hideth not from Thee; but the night shineth as the day: the darkness and the light are both alike to Thee." Psalm 139:12. And with it, another: "The day is Thine, and the night also." Psalm 74:16.

And so, day by day, she sang her songs in the night (Psalm 42:8)—and through it all, she learned that God is an ever-present Help, and that the more she praised Him for the blessings she had, the more she received.

And then, one bright August morning, she learned that a new operation had been developed that might offer hope. Gone now were the old days, when in full sight she walked blindly. Now, she praised her heavenly Father at each step—and submitted all her life and future into His keeping. If the operation would bring healing, then that would be well; but if not, she would continue, unfalteringly, in her trust in God.

And then the operation was performed. And it restored her sight.

Now it was an October morn, and Eva stood by the

kitchen sink. She could see the sparkle of the sunlight in the water, and the brightness of the room shone all about. Before her, through the open window, she could see the bright colors of fall on the trees in the woods outside.

Quietly splitting the early morning mists, rays of sunlight were falling in slanted streaks through the leafy bowers of foliage, and lightening patches of grass, and ground below. It was all a delight to Eva, and she thanked God for it all.

Then, swirling her hand through the dish water, she picked up a large soap bubble and held it to the sunlight. Through it could be seen all the colors of the spectrum in an intermingling of blues and reds, greens, yellows, and violets.

And she remembered the words of the old song:

When thou hast truly thanked thy God
For every blessing sent,
But little time will then remain
For murmur or lament.

Are you and I thanking God for all our blessings? Do we realize that the more we thank Him for all we have, the more we shall have to thank Him for?

There once was an old man in the village who raised songbirds. One day a gentleman stopped by his shop and inquired how he managed to bring such song into the lives of all those little creatures.

"Oh," said he, "their heavenly Father teaches them how to sing.

And when one is not learning his little song well, I place a cover over his cage so that in the dark he can concentrate on it better. Then when he has learned it perfectly I remove the cover, and ever afterward he can sing in the sunlight that which he has learned in the darkness.

For so many of us, it takes the problems of life to bring us to Jesus—who alone can give us happiness.

The children of God are called to be representatives of Christ, showing forth the goodness and mercy of the Lord. As Jesus has revealed to us the true character of the Father, so we are to reveal Christ to a world that does not know His tender, pitying love. "As Thou hast sent Me into the world," said Jesus, "even so have I also sent them into the world." "I in them, and Thou in Me; . . that the world may know that Thou hast sent Me." *John 17: 18, 23*. The apostle Paul says to the disciples of Jesus, "Ye are manifestly declared to be the epistle of Christ," "known and read of all men." *2 Corinthians 3:3, 2*. In every one of His children, Jesus sends a letter to the world. If you are Christ's follower, He sends in you a letter to the family, the village, the street, where you live. Jesus, dwelling in you, desires to speak to the hearts of those who are not acquainted with Him. Perhaps they do not read the Bible or do not hear the voice that speaks to them in its pages; they do not see the love of God through His works. But if you are a true representative of Jesus, it may be that through you they will be led to understand something of His goodness and be won to love and serve Him.

Christians are set as light bearers on the way to heaven. They are to reflect to the world the light shining upon them from Christ. Their life and character should be such that through them others will get a right conception of Christ and of His service.

If we do represent Christ, we shall make His service appear attractive, as it really is. Christians who gather up gloom and sadness to their souls, and murmur and complain, are giving to others a false representation of God and the Christian life. They give the impression that God is not pleased to have His children happy, and in this they bear false witness against our heavenly Father.

Satan is exultant when he can lead the children of God into unbelief and despondency. He delights to see us mistrusting God, doubting His willingness and power to save us. He loves to have us feel that the Lord will do us harm by His providences. It is the work of Satan to represent the Lord as lacking in compassion and pity. He misstates the truth in regard to Him. He fills the imagination with false ideas concerning God; and, instead of dwelling upon the truth in regard to our heavenly Father, we too often fix our minds upon the misrepresentations of Satan and dishonor God by distrusting Him and murmuring against Him. Satan ever seeks to make the religious life one of gloom. He desires it to appear toilsome and difficult; and, when the Christian presents in his own life this view of religion, he is, through his unbelief, seconding the falsehood of Satan.

Dwelling on Themselves

Many, walking along the path of life, dwell upon their mistakes and failures and disappointments, and their hearts are filled with grief and discouragement. While I was in Europe, a sister who had been doing this, and who was in deep distress, wrote to me, asking for some word of encouragement. The night after I had read her letter I dreamed that I was in a garden, and one who seemed to be the owner of the garden was conducting me through its paths. I was gathering the flowers and enjoying their fragrance, when this sister, who had been walking by my side, called my attention to some unsightly briers that were impeding her way. There she was mourning and grieving. She was not walking in the pathway, following the guide, but was walking among the briers and thorns. "Oh," she mourned, "is it not a pity that this beautiful garden is spoiled with thorns?" Then the guide said, "Let the thorns alone, for they will only wound you. Gather the roses, the lilies, and the pinks."

Have there not been some bright spots in your experience? Have you not had some precious seasons when your heart throbbed with joy in response to the Spirit of God? When you look back into the chapters of your life experience do you not find some pleasant pages? Are not God's promises, like the fragrant flowers, growing beside your path on every hand? Will you not let their beauty and sweetness fill your heart with joy?

The briers and thorns will only wound and grieve you; and, if you gather only these things and present them to others, are you not, besides slighting the goodness of God yourself, preventing those around you from walking in the path of life?

It is not wise to gather together all the unpleasant recollections of a past life,—its iniquities and disappointments,—to talk over them and mourn over them until we are overwhelmed with discouragement. A discouraged soul is filled with darkness, shutting out the light of God from his own soul and casting a shadow upon the pathway of others.

Think of the Bright Pictures

Thank God for the bright pictures which He has presented to us. Let us group together the blessed assurances of His love, that we may look upon them continually: The Son of God leaving His Father's throne, clothing His divinity with humanity, that He might rescue man from the power of Satan; His triumph in our behalf, opening heaven to men, revealing to human vision the presence chamber where the Deity unveils His glory; the fallen race uplifted from the pit of ruin into which sin had plunged it and brought again into connection with the infinite God, and having endured the divine test through faith in our Redeemer, clothed in the righteousness of Christ and exalted to His throne—these are the pictures which God would have us contemplate.

When we seem to doubt God's love and distrust His promises we dishonor Him and grieve His Holy Spirit. How would a mother feel if her children were constantly complaining of her, just as though she did not mean them well, when her whole life's effort had been to forward their interests and to give them comfort? Suppose they should doubt her love; it would break her heart. How would any parent feel to be thus treated by his children? And how can our heavenly Father regard us when we distrust His love, which has led Him to give His only begotten Son that we might have life? The apostle writes, "He that spared not His own Son, but delivered Him up for us all, how shall He not with Him also freely give us all things?" *Romans 8:32*. And yet how many, by their actions, if not in word, are saying, "The Lord does not mean this for me. Perhaps He loves others, but He does not love me."

Uttering Words of Doubt

All this is harming your own soul; for every word of doubt you utter is inviting Satan's temptations; it is strengthening in you the tendency to doubt, and it is grieving from you the ministering angels. When Satan tempts you, breathe not a word of doubt or darkness. If you choose to open the door to his suggestions, your mind will be filled with distrust and rebellious questioning. If you talk out your feelings, every doubt you express not only reacts upon yourself, but it is a seed that will germinate and bear fruit in the life of others, and it may be impossible to counteract the influence of your words. You yourself may be able to recover from the season of temptation and from the snare of Satan, but others who have been swayed by your influence may not be able to escape from the unbelief you have suggested. How important that we speak only those things that will give spiritual strength and life!

Angels are listening to hear what kind of report you are bearing to the world about your heavenly Master. Let your conversation be of Him who liveth to make intercession for you before the Father. When you take the hand of a friend, let praise to God be on your lips and in your heart. This will attract his thoughts to Jesus.

All have trials, griefs hard to bear, temptations hard to resist. Do not tell your troubles to your fellow mortals, but carry everything to God in prayer. Make it a rule never to utter one word of doubt or discouragement. You can do much to brighten the life of others and strengthen their efforts, by words of hope and holy cheer.

Do Not Discourage Them

There is many a brave soul sorely pressed by temptation, almost ready to faint in the conflict with self and with the powers of evil. Do not discourage such a one in his hard struggle. Cheer him with brave, hopeful words that shall urge him on his way. Thus the light of Christ may shine from you. "None of us liveth to himself." *Romans 14:7*. By our unconscious influence others may be encouraged and strengthened or they may be discouraged and repelled from Christ and the truth.

There are many who have an erroneous idea of the life and character of Christ. They think that He was devoid of warmth and sunniness, that He was stern, severe, and joyless. In many cases the whole religious experience is colored by these gloomy views.

It is often said that Jesus wept, but that He was never known to smile. Our Saviour was indeed a Man of Sorrows, and acquainted with grief, for He opened His heart to all the woes of men. But though His life was self-denying and shadowed with pain and care, His spirit was not crushed. His countenance did not wear an expression of grief and repining, but ever one of peaceful serenity. His heart was a wellspring of life and, wherever He went, He carried rest and peace, joy and gladness.

Our Saviour was deeply serious and intensely in earnest, but never gloomy or morose. The life of those who imitate Him will be full of earnest purpose; they will have a deep sense of personal responsibility. Levity will be repressed; there will be no boisterous merriment, no rude jesting; but the religion of Jesus gives peace like a river. It does not quench the light of joy; it does not restrain cheerfulness nor cloud the sunny, smiling face. Christ came not to be ministered unto but to minister; and when His love reigns in the heart, we shall follow His example.

Dwell on His Love

If we keep uppermost in our minds the unkind and unjust acts of others we shall find it impossible to love them as Christ has loved us; but if our thoughts dwell upon the wondrous love and pity of Christ for us, the same spirit will flow out to others. We should love and respect one another, notwithstanding the faults and imperfections that we cannot help seeing. Humility and self-distrust should be cultivated, and a patient tenderness with the faults of others. This will kill out all narrowing selfishness and make us large-hearted and generous.

The psalmist says, "Trust in the Lord, and do good; so shalt thou dwell in the land, and verily thou shalt be fed."

Psalm 37:3. "Trust in the Lord." Each day has its burdens, its cares and perplexities; and, when we meet how ready we are to talk of our difficulties and trials. So many borrowed troubles intrude, so many fears are indulged, such a weight of anxiety is expressed, that one might suppose we had no pitying, loving Saviour ready to hear all our requests and to be to us a present help in every time of need.

Some are always fearing, and borrowing trouble. Every day they are surrounded with the tokens of God's love; every day they are enjoying the bounties of His providence; but they overlook these present blessings. Their minds are continually dwelling upon something disagreeable which they fear may come; or some difficulty may really exist which, though small, blinds their eyes to the many things that demand gratitude. The difficulties they encounter, instead of driving them to God, the only source of their help, separate them from Him because they awaken unrest and repining.

Do we well to be thus unbelieving? Why should we be ungrateful and distrustful? Jesus is our friend; all heaven is interested in our welfare. We should not allow the perplexities and worries of everyday life to fret the mind and cloud the brow. If we do we shall always have something to vex and annoy. We should not indulge a solicitude that only frets and wears us, but does not help us to bear trials.

God Can Solve Your Problems

You may be perplexed in business; your prospects may grow darker and darker, and you may be threatened with loss; but do not become discouraged; cast your care upon God, and remain calm and cheerful. Pray for wisdom to manage your affairs with direction, and thus prevent loss and disaster. Do all you can on your part to bring about favorable results. Jesus has promised His aid, but not apart from our effort. When, relying upon our Helper, you have done all you can, accept the result cheerfully.

It is not the will of God that His people should be weighed down with care. But our Lord does not deceive us. He does not say to us, "Do not fear; there are no dangers in your path." He knows there are trials and dangers, and He deals with us plainly. He does not propose to take His people out of a world of sin and evil, but He points them to a never-failing refuge. His prayer for His disciples was, "I pray not that Thou shouldest take them out of the world, but that Thou shouldest keep them from the evil." *John 17:15-16*. "In the world," He says, "ye shall have tribulation: but be of good cheer; I have overcome the world" (*John 16:33*).

In His Sermon on the Mount, Christ taught His disciples precious lessons in regard to the necessity of trusting in God. These lessons were designed to encourage the children of God through all ages, and they have come down to our time full of instruction and comfort. The Saviour pointed His followers to the birds of the air as they warbled their carols of praise, unencumbered with thoughts of care, for "they sow not, neither do they reap." And yet the great Father provides for their needs. The Saviour asks, "Are ye not much better than they?" *Matthew 6:26*. The great Provider for man and beast opens His hand and supplies all His creatures. The birds of the air are not beneath His notice. He does not drop the food into their bills, but He makes provision for their needs. They must gather the grains He has scattered for them. They must prepare the material for their little nests. They must feed their young. They go forth singing to their labor, for "your heavenly Father feedeth them." And "are ye not much better than they?" Are not you, as intelligent, spiritual worshipers, of more value than the birds of the air? Will not the Author of our being, the Preserver of our life, the One who formed us in His own divine image, provide for our necessities if we but trust in Him?

The Little Things of Nature Will Tell You

Christ pointed His disciples to the flowers of the field, growing in rich profusion and glowing in the simple beauty which the heavenly Father had given them, as an expression of His love to man. He said, "Consider the lilies of the field, how they grow." The beauty and simplicity of these natural flowers far outrival the splendor of Solomon. The most gorgeous attire produced by the skill of art cannot bear comparison with the natural grace and radiant beauty of the flowers of God's creation. Jesus asks, "If God so clothe the grass of the field, which today is, and tomorrow is cast into the oven, shall He not much more clothe you, O ye of little faith?" *Matthew 6:28, 30.* If God, the divine Artist, gives to the simple flowers that perish in a day their delicate and varied colors, how much greater care will He have for those who are created in His own image? This lesson of Christ's is a rebuke to the anxious thought, the perplexity and doubt, of the faithless heart.

The Lord would have all His sons and daughters happy, peaceful, and obedient. Jesus says, "My peace I give unto you: not as the world giveth, give I unto you. Let not your heart be troubled, neither let it be afraid." *John 14:27.* "These things have I spoken unto you, that My joy might remain in you, and that your joy might be full." *John 15:11.*

Happiness that is sought from selfish motives, outside of the path of duty, is ill-balanced, fitful, and transitory; it passes away, and the soul is filled with loneliness and sorrow; but there is joy and satisfaction in the service of God. The Christian is not left to walk in uncertain paths; he is not left to vain regrets and disappointments. If we do not have the pleasures of this life we may still be joyful in looking to the life beyond.

A Fullness of Joy

But even here Christians may have the joy of communion with Christ; they may have the light of His love, the perpetual comfort of His presence. Every step in life may bring us closer to Jesus, may give us a deeper experience of His love, and may bring us one step nearer to the blessed home of peace. Then let us not cast away our confidence, but have firm assurance, firmer than ever before. "Hitherto hath the Lord helped us" (*1 Samuel 7:12*), and He will help us to the end. Let us look to the monumental pillars, reminders of what the Lord has done to comfort us and to save us from the hand of the destroyer. Let us keep fresh in our memory all the tender mercies that God has shown us,—the tears He has wiped away, the pains He has soothed, the anxieties removed, the fears dispelled, the wants supplied, the blessings bestowed,—thus strengthening ourselves for all that is before us through the remainder of our pilgrimage.

We cannot but look forward to new perplexities in the coming conflict, but we may look on what is past as well as on what is to come, and say, "Hitherto hath the Lord helped us." "As thy days, so shall thy strength be." *Deuteronomy 33:25.* The trial will not exceed the strength that shall be given us to bear it. Then let us take up our work just where we find it, believing that whatever may come, strength proportionate to the trial will be given.

When the Gates Are Opened

And by and by the gates of heaven will be thrown open to admit God's children and, from the lips of the King of glory the benediction will fall on their ears like richest music, "Come, ye blessed of My Father, inherit the kingdom prepared for you from the foundation of the world." *Matthew 25:34.*

Then the redeemed will be welcomed to the home that Jesus is preparing for them. There their companions will not be the vile of earth, liars, idolaters, the impure, and unbelieving; but they will associate with those who have overcome Satan and through divine grace have formed perfect characters. Every sinful tendency, every imperfection, that afflicts them here has been removed by the blood of Christ, and the excellence and brightness of His glory, far exceeding the brightness of the sun, is imparted to them. And the moral beauty, the perfection of His character, shines through them, in worth far exceeding this outward splendor. They are without fault before the great white throne, sharing the dignity and the privileges of the angels.

In view of the glorious inheritance that may be his, "what shall a man give in exchange for his soul?" He may be poor, yet he possesses in himself a wealth and dignity that the world could never bestow. The soul redeemed and cleansed from sin, with all its noble powers, dedicated to the service of God, is of surpassing worth; and there is joy in heaven in the presence of God and the holy angels over one soul redeemed, a joy that is expressed in songs of holy triumph.

BIBLE PROMISES YOU CAN USE

Unto the upright there ariseth light in the darkness.
– Psalm 112:4.

Thou hast been a strength to the poor, a strength to the needy in his distress, a refuge from the storm, a shadow from the heat, when the blast of the terrible ones is as a storm against the wall. *– Isaiah 25:4.*

O Lord, my strength and my fortress and my refuge in the day of affliction. *– Jeremiah 16:19.*

When I fall, I shall arise; when I sit in darkness, the Lord shall be a light unto me. *– Micah 7:8-9.*

The Lord is good, a stronghold in the day of trouble; and He knoweth them that trust in Him. *– Nahum 1:7.*

Come unto Me, all ye that labour and are heavy laden, and I will give you rest. *– Matthew 11:28.*

These things I have spoken unto you, that in Me ye might have peace. In the world ye shall have tribulation; but be of good cheer: I have overcome the world. *– John 16:33.*

For as the sufferings of Christ abound in us, so our consolation also aboundeth by Christ. *– 2 Corinthians 1:5.*

If thou wilt diligently hearken to the voice of the Lord thy God, and wilt do that which is right in His sight, and wilt give ear to His commandments, and keep all His statutes, I will put none of these diseases upon thee. *– Exodus 15:26.*

Surely He shall deliver thee from the snare of the fowler, and from the noisome pestilence. *– Psalm 91:3.*

Who forgiveth all thine iniquities; who healeth all thy diseases. *– Psalm 103:3.*

Thou shalt not be afraid for the terror by night, nor for the arrow that flieth by day. *– Psalm 91:5.*

The Lord preserveth the simple: I was brought low, and He helped me. *– Psalm 116:6.*

Cast me not off in the time of old age; forsake me not when my strength faileth. *– Psalm 71:9.*

CHAPTER FOURTEEN

How Sin Entered the Universe

"Mr. Finney," the young man said, "I don't really believe there is a devil." The preacher looked at him keenly for a moment, and replied: "Don't you, now? Well, you really resist him for awhile in your own strength, and you'll soon change your views."

Griffith Thomas tells of a man who was a slave to drink. Nothing that he nor his friends did could get him away from it. Then he found Christ—and was freed from that terrible curse. Someone asked him how this wondrous change had come about.

"Why, Hank, you must have gotten the mastery of the devil at last?" "No," he said, "but I have got the Master of the devil." Since Satan is a supernatural enemy, it takes a supernatural power to overcome him. That power is Christ. He not only can forgive your sins, but He can enable you to conquer them.

Ike Miller was the terror of a North England mining district. Then gospel meetings began at the old church as the young preacher, Henry Moorhouse, began talking on the love of Jesus for a lost world. Ike Miller had said that he would break up the series of meetings. With this in mind, he walked in and took his seat

near the front. Everyone in the room feared what would happen there that night.

A disturbance was indeed created, but it was in the depths of Ike's soul. Moorhouse told about the fall of man and God's plan to enable him to obey God—by sending Jesus to die for his sins. Quietly, Ike listened to the story of Calvary and a Saviour's love.

Just as the meeting was closing, Ike got up alone and walked out suddenly. Afterward, several told the young preacher that, with Ike there, he should have spoken about the final reward for sin. "What will he care about the love of Christ?" they said.

Meanwhile, Ike was walking home. Part way there, he turned off the path into a wood, got down on his knees and cried to God and asked Him for forgiveness—for help to live a different life. He remained there till the peace and forgiveness of God came.

Striding up to the door of his home, he opened it in a burst. One of the children gave a muffled gasp and ran behind his mother. The other peeked from behind a doorway to see what would happen next.

His wife said nervously, "Home so early?" Then she paused to see what Ike's response would be.

To her astonishment, she saw that he was not drunk but perfectly sober,—and more, he was crying!

To her greater astonishment, he walked over to her, put his arms around her and kissed her.

"Lass," he said, "God has brought your husband back to you."

Then, sitting on a chair, he called the children to him. Slowly, hesitantly, they came. He enfolded them in his arms and told them that he had given his heart to Jesus, and he asked their forgiveness. Together they wept, and he told them that from now on, life would be different.

And it was, for Ike quickly discovered that Christianity is more than a single surrender;—it is a lifelong walk with Jesus that begins anew each morning with Bible study, prayer, and renewed dedication.

Before the entrance of evil, there was peace and joy throughout the universe. All was in perfect harmony with the Creator's will. Love for God was supreme, love for one another impartial. Christ the Word, the only begotten of God, was one with the eternal Father, one in nature, in character, and in purpose , the only being in all the universe that could enter into all the counsels and purposes of God. By Christ, the Father wrought in the creation of all heavenly beings. "By him were all things created, that are in Heaven, . . whether they be thrones, or dominions, or principalities, or powers . ." *Colossians 1:16*. And to Christ, equally with the Father, all Heaven gave allegiance. The law of love being the foundation of the government of God, the happiness of all created beings depended upon their perfect accord with its great principles of righteousness. God desires from all His creatures the service of love, homage that springs from an intelligent appreciation of His character. He takes no pleasure in a forced allegiance, and to all He grants freedom of will, that they may render Him voluntary service.

How Sin Began

But there was one that chose to pervert this freedom. Sin originated with him, who, next to Christ, had been most honored of God, and who stood highest in power and glory among the inhabitants of Heaven. Before his fall, Lucifer was first of the covering cherubs, holy and undefiled. "Thus saith the Lord God; Thou sealest up the sum full of wisdom and perfect in beauty. Thou has been in Eden the garden of God; every precious stone was thy covering . . Thou art the anointed cherub that covereth; and I have set thee so; thou wast upon the holy mountain of God; thou hast walked up and down in the midst of the stones of fire. Thou wast perfect in thy ways from the day that thou was created, till iniquity was found in thee." *Ezekiel 28:12-15*.

Lucifer might have remained in favor with God, beloved and honored by all the angelic host, exercising his noble powers to bless others and to glorify his Maker. But, says the prophet, "Thine heart was lifted up because of thy beauty, thou hast corrupted thy wisdom by reason of thy brightness

. ." *Ezekiel 28:17*. Little by little, Lucifer came to indulge a desire for self-exaltation. "Thou hast set thine heart as the heart of God." *Verse 6*. "Thou hast said: . . I will exalt my throne above the stars of God; I will sit also upon the mount of the congregation, . . I will ascend above the heights of the clouds; I will be like the Most High." *Isa. 14:13-14*. Instead of seeking to make God supreme m the affections and allegiance of His creatures, it was Lucifer's endeavor to win their service and homage to himself. And, coveting the honor which the infinite Father had bestowed upon His Son, this prince of angels aspired to power which it was the prerogative of Christ alone to wield.

They Pleaded with Him

All Heaven had rejoiced to reflect the Creator's glory and to show forth His praise. And while God was thus honored, all had been peace and gladness; but a note of discord now marred the celestial harmonies. The service and exaltation of self, contrary to the Creator's plan, awakened forebodings of evil in minds to whom God's glory was supreme. The heavenly councils pleaded with Lucifer. The Son of God presented before him the greatness, the goodness, and the justice of the Creator, and the sacred, unchanging nature of His law. God Himself had established the order of Heaven; and, in departing from it, Lucifer would dishonor his Maker and bring ruin upon himself. But the warning, given in infinite love and mercy, only aroused a spirit of resistance. Lucifer allowed jealousy of Christ to prevail, and he became the more determined.

Pride in his own glory nourished the desire for supremacy. The high honors conferred upon Lucifer were not appreciated as the gift of God, and called forth no gratitude to the Creator. He gloried in his brightness and exaltation, and aspired to be equal with God. He was beloved and reverenced by the heavenly host. Angels delighted to execute his commands, and he was clothed with wisdom and glory above them all. Yet the Son of God was the acknowledged sovereign of Heaven, one in power and authority with the Father. In all the counsels of God, Christ was a participant while

Lucifer was not permitted thus to enter into the divine purposes. "Why," questioned this mighty angel, "should Christ have the supremacy? Why is He thus honored above Lucifer?"

Opposed to God's Law

Leaving his place in the immediate presence of God, Lucifer went forth to diffuse the spirit of discontent among the angels. Working with mysterious secrecy, and for a time concealing his real purpose under an appearance of reverence for God, he endeavored to excite dissatisfaction concerning the laws that governed heavenly beings, intimating that they imposed an unnecessary restraint. Since their natures were holy, he urged that the angels should obey the dictates of their own will. He sought to create sympathy for himself, by representing that God had dealt unjustly with him in bestowing supreme honor upon Christ. He claimed that in aspiring to greater power and honor he was not aiming at self-exaltation, but was seeking to secure liberty for all the inhabitants of Heaven, that by this means they might attain to a higher state of existence.

God, in His great mercy, bore long with Lucifer. He was not immediately degraded from his exalted station when he first indulged the spirit of discontent, nor even when he began to present his false claims before the loyal angels. Long was he retained in Heaven. Again and again he was offered pardon, on condition of repentance and submission. Such efforts as only infinite love and wisdom could devise, were made to convince him of his error. The spirit of discontent had never before been known in Heaven. Lucifer himself did not at first see whither he was drifting; he did not understand the real nature of his feelings. But as his dissatisfaction was proved to be without cause, Lucifer was convinced that he was in the wrong, that the divine claims were just, and that he ought to acknowledge them as such before all Heaven. Had he done this, he might have saved himself and many angels. He had not at this time fully cast off his allegiance to God. Though he had forsaken his position as covering cherub, yet if he had been willing to return to God, acknowledging the Creator's wisdom, and satisfied to fill the place appointed him in God's great plan, he would have been reinstated in his office. But pride forbade him to submit. He persistently defended his own course, maintained that he had no need of repentance, and fully committed himself, in the great controversy, against his Maker.

A Master at Deception

All the powers of his mastermind were now bent to the work of deception, to secure the sympathy of the angels that had been under his command. Even the fact that Christ had warned and counseled him, was perverted to serve his traitorous designs. To those whose loving trust bound them most closely to him, Satan had represented that he was wrongly judged, that his position was not respected, and that his liberty was to be abridged. From misrepresentation of the words of Christ, he passed to prevarication and direct falsehood, accusing the Son of God of a design to humiliate him before the inhabitants of Heaven. He sought also to make a false issue between himself and the loyal angels. All whom he could not subvert and bring fully to his side, he accused of indifference to the interests of heavenly beings. The very work which he himself was doing, he charged upon those who remained true to God. And to sustain his charge of God's injustice toward him, he resorted to misrepresentation of the words and acts of the Creator. It was his policy to perplex the angels with subtle arguments concerning the purposes of God. Everything that was simple he shrouded in mystery, and by artful perversion cast doubt upon the plainest statements of Jehovah. His high position, in such close connection with the divine administration, gave greater force to his representations, and many were induced to unite with him in rebellion against Heaven's authority.

It Takes Time

God in His wisdom permitted Satan to carry forward his work, until the spirit of disaffection ripened into active revolt. It was necessary for his plans to be fully developed, that their true nature and tendency might be seen by all. Lucifer, as the anointed cherub, had been highly exalted; he was greatly loved by the heavenly beings, and his influence over them was strong. God's government included not only the inhabitants of Heaven, but of all the worlds that He had created; and Satan thought that if he could carry the angels of Heaven with him in rebellion, he could carry also the other worlds. He had artfully presented his side of the question, employing sophistry and fraud to secure his objects. His power to deceive was very great, and by disguising himself in a cloak of falsehood he had gained an advantage. Even the loyal angels could not fully discern his character, or see to what his work was leading.

Satan had been so highly honored, and all his acts were so clothed with mystery, that it was difficult to disclose to the angels the true nature of his work. Until fully developed, sin would not appear the evil thing it was. Heretofore it had no place in the universe of God, and holy beings had no conception of its nature and malignity. They could not discern the terrible consequences that would result from setting aside the divine law. Satan had, at first, concealed his work under a specious profession of loyalty to God. He claimed to be seeking to promote the honor of God, the stability of his government, and the good of all the inhabitants of Heaven. While instilling discontent into the minds of the angels under him, he had artfully made it appear that he was seeking to remove dissatisfaction. When he urged that changes be made in the order and laws of God's government, it was under the pretense that these were necessary in order to preserve harmony in Heaven.

In His dealing with sin, God could employ only righteousness and truth. Satan could use what God could not—flattery and deceit. He had sought to falsify the word of God, and had misrepresented His plan of government before the angels, claiming that God was not just in laying laws and rules upon the inhabitants of Heaven; that in requiring submission and obedience from His creatures, He was seeking merely the exaltation of Himself. Therefore it must be demonstrated before the inhabitants of Heaven as well as of all the worlds, that God's government was just, His law perfect.

Satan had made it appear that he himself was seeking to promote the good of the universe. The true character of the usurper, and his real object, must be understood by all. He must have time to manifest himself by his wicked works.

Our Work Will Condemn

The discord which his own course had caused in Heaven, Satan charged upon the law and government of God. All evil he declared to be the result of the divine administration. He claimed that it was his own object to improve upon the statutes of Jehovah. Therefore it was necessary that he should demonstrate the nature of his claims, and show the working out of his proposed changes in the divine law. His own work must condemn him. Satan had claimed from the first that he was not in rebellion. The whole universe must see the deceiver unmasked.

Even when it was decided that he could no longer remain in Heaven, infinite wisdom did not destroy Satan. Since the service of love can alone be acceptable to God, the allegiance of His creatures must rest upon a conviction of His justice and benevolence. The inhabitants of Heaven and of other worlds, being unprepared to comprehend the nature or consequences of sin, could not then have seen the justice and mercy of God in the destruction of Satan. Had he been immediately blotted from existence, they would have served God from fear rather than from love. The influence of the deceiver would not have been fully destroyed, nor would the spirit of rebellion have been utterly eradicated. Evil must be permitted to come to maturity. For the good of the entire universe through ceaseless ages, Satan must more fully develop his principles, that his charges against the divine government might be seen in their true light by all created beings, that the justice and mercy of God and the immutability of His law might forever be placed beyond all question.

A Lesson for All Time

Satan's rebellion was to be a lesson to the universe through all coming ages, a perpetual testimony to the nature and terrible results of sin. The working out of Satan's rule, its effects upon both men and angels, would show what must be the fruit of setting aside the divine authority. It would testify that with the existence of God's government and His law is bound up the well-being of all the creatures He has made. Thus the history of his terrible experiment of rebellion was to be a perpetual safeguard to all holy intelligences, to prevent them from being deceived as to the nature of transgression, to save them from committing sin, and suffering its punishment.

To the very close of the controversy in Heaven, the great usurper continued to justify himself. When it was announced that with all his sympathizers he must be expelled from the abodes of bliss, then the rebel leader boldly avowed his contempt for the Creator's law. He reiterated his claim that angels needed no control, but should be left to follow their own will, which would ever guide them right. He denounced the divine statutes as a restriction of their liberty, and declared that it was his purpose to secure the abolition of law; that, freed from this restraint, the hosts of Heaven might enter upon a more exalted, more glorious state of existence.

Cast Out of Heaven

With one accord, Satan and his host threw the blame of their rebellion wholly upon Christ, declaring that if they had not been reproved they would never have rebelled. Thus stubborn and defiant in their disloyalty, seeking vainly to overthrow the government of God, yet blasphemously claiming to be themselves the innocent victims of oppressive power, the arch-rebel and all his sympathizers were at last banished from Heaven.

The same spirit that prompted rebellion in Heaven, still inspires rebellion on earth. Satan has continued with men the same policy which he pursued with the angels. His spirit now reigns in the children of disobedience. Like him they seek to break down the restraints of the law of God, and promise men liberty through transgression of its precepts. Reproof of sin still arouses the spirit of hatred and resistance. When God's messages of warning are brought home to the conscience, Satan leads men to justify themselves and to seek the sympathy of others in their course of sin. Instead of correcting their errors, they excite indignation against the reprover, as if he were the sole cause of difficulty. From the days of righteous Abel to our own time, such is the spirit which has been displayed toward those who dare to condemn sin.

Methods Unchanged

By the same misrepresentation of the character of God as he had practiced in Heaven, causing Him to be regarded as severe and tyrannical, Satan induced man to sin. And having succeeded thus far, he declared that God's unjust restrictions had led to man's fall, as they had led to his own rebellion.

But the Eternal One Himself proclaims His character: "The Lord God, merciful and gracious, long-suffering, and abundant in goodness and truth, keeping mercy for thousands, forgiving iniquity and transgression and sin, and that will by no means clear the guilty." *Exodus 34:6-7.* In the banishment of Satan from Heaven, God declared His justice and maintained the honor of His throne. But when man had sinned through yielding to the deceptions of this apostate spirit, God gave an evidence of His love by yielding up His only begotten Son to die for the fallen race. In the atonement the character of God is revealed. The mighty argument of the cross demonstrates to the whole universe that the course of sin which Lucifer had chosen was in nowise chargeable upon the government of God.

Behold What Love and Hate

In the contest between Christ and Satan, during the Saviour's earthly ministry, the character of the great deceiver was unmasked. Nothing could so effectually have uprooted Satan from the affections of the heavenly angels and the whole loyal universe as did his cruel warfare upon the world's Redeemer. The daring blasphemy of his demand that Christ should pay him homage, his presumptuous boldness in bearing Him to the mountain summit and the pinnacle of the temple, the malicious intent betrayed in urging Him to cast Himself down from the dizzy height, the unsleeping malice that hunted Him from place to place, inspiring the hearts of priests and people to reject His love, and at the last to cry, "Crucify Him! Crucify Him!" All this excited the amazement and indignation of the universe.

It was Satan that prompted the world's rejection of Christ. The prince of evil exerted all his power and cunning to destroy Jesus; for he saw that the Saviour's mercy and love, His compassion and pitying tenderness, were representing to the world the character of God. Satan contested every claim put forth by the Son of God, and employed men as his agents to fill the Saviour's life with suffering and sorrow. The sophistry and falsehood by which he had sought to hinder the work of Jesus, the hatred manifested through the children of disobedience, his cruel accusations against Him whose life was one of exemplary goodness, all sprang from deep-seated revenge. The pent-up fires of envy and malice, hatred and revenge, burst forth on Calvary against the Son of God while all Heaven gazed upon the scene in silent horror.

When the great sacrifice had been consummated, Christ ascended on high, refusing the adoration of angels until He had presented the request, "I will that they also, whom Thou hast given Me, be with Me where I am." *John 17:24*. Then with inexpressible love and power came forth the answer from the Father's throne, "Let all the angels of God worship Him." *Hebrews 1:6*. Not a stain rested upon Jesus. His humiliation ended, His sacrifice completed; there was given unto Him a name that is above every name.

Selfishness Unmasked

Now the guilt of Satan stood forth without excuse. He had revealed his true character as a liar and a murderer. It was seen that the very same spirit with which he ruled the children of men, who were under his power, he would have manifested had he been permitted to control the inhabitants of Heaven. He had claimed that the transgression of God's law would bring liberty and exaltation; but it was seen to result in bondage and degradation.

Satan's lying charges against the divine character and government appeared in their true light. He had accused God of seeking merely the exaltation of Himself in requiring submission and obedience from His creatures, and had declared that while the Creator exacted self-denial, and made others, He Himself practiced no self-denial, and made no sacrifice. Now it was seen that for the salvation of a fallen and sinful race, the Ruler of the universe had made the greatest sacrifice which love could make; for "God was in Christ, reconciling the world unto Himself." *2 Corinthians 5:19*. It was seen, also, that while Lucifer had opened the door for the entrance of sin, by his desire for honor and supremacy, Christ had, in order to destroy sin, humbled Himself, and become obedient unto death.

What God Is Like

God had manifested His abhorrence of the principles of rebellion. All Heaven saw His justice revealed, both in the condemnation of Satan and in the redemption of man. Lucifer had declared that if the law of God was changeless, and its penalty could not be remitted, every transgressor must be forever debarred from the Creator's favor. He had claimed that the sinful race were placed beyond redemption, and were therefore his rightful prey. But the death of Christ was an argument in man's behalf that could not be overthrown. The penalty of the law fell upon Him who was equal with God, and man was free to accept the righteousness of Christ; and by a life of penitence and humiliation to triumph, as the Son of God had triumphed over the power of Satan. Thus God is just, and yet the justifier of all who believe in Jesus.

But it was not merely to accomplish the redemption of man that Christ came to the earth to suffer and die. He came to "magnify the law" and to "make it honorable." Not alone that the inhabitants of this world might regard the law as it should be regarded; but it was to demonstrate to all the worlds of the universe that God's law is unchangeable. Could its claims have been set aside, then the Son of God need not have yielded up His life to atone for its transgression. The death of Christ proves it immutable. And the sacrifice to which infinite love impelled the Father and the Son, that sinners might be redeemed, demonstrates to all the universe—what nothing less than this plan of atonement could have sufficed to do—that justice and mercy are the foundation of the law and government of God.

It Will End in Ashes

In the final execution of the Judgment it will be seen that no cause for sin exists. When the Judge of all the earth shall demand of Satan, "Why hast thou rebelled against Me, and robbed Me of the subjects of My kingdom?" the originator of evil can render no excuse. Every mouth will be stopped, and all the hosts of rebellion will be speechless. The cross of Calvary, while it declares the law immutable, proclaims to the universe that the wages of sin is death. In the Saviour's expiring cry, "It is finished," the death-knell of Satan was rung. The great controversy which had been so long in progress was then decided, and the final eradication of evil was made certain. The Son of God passed through the portals of the tomb, that "through death He might destroy him that had the power of death, that is, the devil." *Hebrews 2:14*. Lucifer's desire for self-exaltation had led him to say, "1 will exalt my throne above the stars of God . . I will be like the Most High." God declares, "I will bring thee to ashes upon the earth, . . and never shalt thou be any more." *Isaiah 14:13-14; Ezekiel 28:18-19*. When "the day cometh that shall burn as an oven" . . "all the proud, yea, and all that do wickedly, shall be stubble; and the day that cometh shall burn them up, saith the Lord of hosts, that it shall leave them neither root nor branch." *Malachi 4:1*.

Eternally Secure

The whole universe will have become witnesses to the nature and results of sin. And its utter extermination, which in the beginning would have brought fear to angels and dishonor to God, will now vindicate His love and establish His honor before a universe of beings who delight to do His will, and in whose heart is His law. Never will evil again be manifest. Says the Word of God, "Affliction shall not rise up the second time." *Nahum 1:9*. The law of God, which Satan has reproached as the yoke of bondage, will be honored as the law of liberty. A tested and proved creation will never again be turned from allegiance to Him whose character has been fully manifested before them as fathomless love and infinite wisdom.

Discovery

To many minds, the origin of sin and the reason for its existence are a source of great perplexity. They see the work of evil, with its terrible results of woe and desolation, and they question how all this can exist under the sovereignty of One who is infinite in wisdom, in power, and in love. Here is a mystery, of which they find no explanation. And in their uncertainty and doubt, they are blinded to truths plainly revealed in God's Word, and essential to salvation. There are those who, in their inquiries concerning the existence of sin, endeavor to search into that which God has never revealed; hence they find no solution of their difficulties; and such as are actuated by a disposition to doubt and cavil seize upon this as an excuse for rejecting the words of Holy Writ. Others, however, fail of a satisfactory understanding of the great problem of evil, from the fact that tradition and misinterpretation have obscured the teaching of the Bible concerning the character of God, the nature of His government, and the principles of His dealing with sin.

It is impossible to so explain the origin of sin as to give a reason for its existence. Yet enough may be understood concerning both the origin and the final disposition of sin, to fully make manifest the justice and benevolence of God in all His dealings with evil. Nothing is more plainly taught in Scripture than that God was in nowise responsible for the entrance of sin; that there was no arbitrary withdrawal of divine grace, no deficiency in the divine government, that gave occasion for the uprising of rebellion. Sin is an intruder, for whose presence no reason can be given. It is mysterious, unaccountable; to excuse it, is to defend it. Could excuse for it be found, or cause be shown for its existence, it would cease to be sin. Our only definition of sin is that given in the Word of God; it is "the transgression of the law." It is the outworking of a principle at war with the great law of love which is the foundation of the divine government.

CHAPTER FIFTEEN

The 2000-Year Prophecy of Christ

Madam Guyon (pronounced Gay-yo) was born of wealthy parentage in Montargis, France, about fifty miles north of Paris, in the year 1648. At the age of ten, she found a Bible and earnestly studied it for several months, to the exclusion of everything else. But at the age of twelve, she gave up Christianity and eventually grew into a beautiful—but vain and proud—society "butterfly." Her wealthy mother indulged her desire for an abundance of clothes and parties.

Following a visit by De Tossi, a cousin of hers who was on his way to China as a missionary, she became deeply convicted of her duty to return to God, and she began trying to live a Christian life. But she did not come to the point of surrendering to Christ; and, after several months, she again returned to her worldliness. Then her family moved to Paris. Beautiful and very intelligent, she eventually married a man of great wealth who was twenty-two years older than she.

But it was not a happy marriage. Sickness, the death

of loved ones, the loss of much of the family wealth, quarreling relatives,—all brought sorrows of many kinds. Bitterly had she learned that she could find rest nowhere except in God, and she again sought Him earnestly.

Although now a mother of several children, she began studying the Word of God whenever possible, and she started sharing her faith with all whom she met. Gradually, amid continued trials and problems, she acquired a very deep Christian experience as she kept reading, praying, and obeying the Scriptures.

But on a trip to Paris, enjoyment of old friends lowered her standards again,—and then came a terrible attack of smallpox which totally destroyed her beauty.

Though more problems and difficulties were later to follow, she now clung to Christ as her only hope in this life and for the next. Continually her experience in the Christ-life deepened.

With the passing of time, her influence widened as she told others and still others how to come to Christ and walk closely with Him day by day.

Wherever she went in France, a revival of religion began as others sought to live more dedicated lives. So many were helped that priests, church leaders, and even university professors became fearful of losing their own influence over the people. Finally, the Church convinced Louis XIV, the King of France, that she was too dangerous to have around.

By order of the king, Madam Guyon was imprisoned; but, while there, she wrote books which were circulated all over the country. Later released, she was again imprisoned in 1695, and finally died in 1717 at the age of 69 years.

Thousands in France were helped by her life and her more than thirty books. Madam Guyon was but one of millions, down through the Dark Ages and afterward, who were persecuted and slain for the crime of being a Christian and living by the Bible.

"If thou hadst known, even thou, at least in this thy day, the things which belong unto thy peace! but now they are hid from thine eyes. For the days shall come upon thee, that thine enemies shall cast a trench about thee, and compass thee round, and keep thee in on every side, and shall lay thee even with the ground, and thy children within thee; and they shall not leave in thee one stone upon another; because thou knewest not the time of thy visitation." *Luke 19:42-44.*

The disciples had been filled with awe and wonder at Christ's prediction of the overthrow of the temple, and they desired to understand more fully the meaning of His words. The Lord had told them that He would come the second time. Hence at the mention of judgments upon Jerusalem, their minds reverted to that coming, and as they were gathered about the Saviour upon the Mount of Olives, they asked, "When shall these things be? and what shall be the sign of thy coming, and of the end of the world?" *Matthew 24:3.*

Prophecy of the End

The future was mercifully veiled from the disciples. Had they at that time fully comprehended the two awful facts,—the Redeemer's sufferings and death and the destruction of their city and temple—they would have been overwhelmed with horror. Christ presented before them an outline of the prominent events to take place before the close of time. His words were not then fully understood; but their meaning was to be unfolded as His people should need the instruction therein given. The prophecy which He uttered was twofold in its meaning: while foreshadowing the destruction of Jerusalem, it prefigured also the terrors of the last great day. Jesus declared to the listening disciples the judgments that were to fall upon apostate Israel, and especially the retributive vengeance that would come upon them for their rejection and crucifixion of the Messiah. Unmistakable signs would precede the awful climax.

A Symbol of the World

Christ saw in Jerusalem a symbol of the world hardened in unbelief and rebellion, and hastening on to meet the retributive judgments of God. The woes of a fallen race, pressing upon His soul, forced from His lips that exceeding bitter cry. He saw the record of sin traced in human misery, tears, and blood; His heart was moved with infinite pity for the afflicted and suffering ones of earth; He yearned to relieve them all. But even His hand might not turn back the tide of human woe; few would seek their only source of help. He was willing to pour out His soul unto death, to bring salvation within their reach; but few would come to Him that they might have life.

The Majesty of Heaven in tears! The Son of the infinite God, troubled in spirit, bowed down with anguish! The scene filled all Heaven with wonder. That scene reveals to us the exceeding sinfulness of sin; it shows how hard a task it is, even for infinite power, to save the guilty from the consequences of transgressing the law of God. Jesus, looking down to the last generation, saw the world involved in a deception similar to that which caused the destruction of Jerusalem. The great sin of the Jews was their rejection of Christ; the great sin of the Christian world would be their rejection of the law of God, the foundation of His government in Heaven and earth. The precepts of Jehovah would be despised and set at naught. Millions in bondage to sin, slaves of Satan, doomed to suffer the second death, would refuse to listen to the words of truth in their day of visitation. Terrible blindness! Strange infatuation!

Another Fulfillment

The Saviour's prophecy concerning the visitation of judgments upon Jerusalem is to have another fulfillment, of which that terrible desolation was but a faint shadow. In the fate of the chosen city we may behold the doom of a world that has rejected God's mercy and trampled upon His law. Dark are the records of human misery that earth has witnessed during its long centuries of crime. The heart sickens and the mind grows faint in contemplation. Terrible have been the results of rejecting the authority of Heaven. But a scene yet darker is presented in the revelation of the future. The records of the past,—the long procession of tumults, conflicts, and revolutions, the "battle of the warrior is with confused noise, and garments rolled in blood." *Isaiah 9:5.* What are these, in contrast with the terrors of that day when the restraining Spirit of God shall be wholly withdrawn from the wicked, no longer to hold in check the outbursts of human passion and satanic wrath! The world will then behold, as never before, the results of Satan's rule.

As the Midnight Thief

The world is no more ready to credit the message for this time than were the Jews to receive the Saviour's warning concerning Jerusalem. Come when it may, the day of God will come unawares to the ungodly. When life is going on in its unvarying round; when men are absorbed in pleasure, in business, in traffic, in money-making; when the religious leaders are magnifying the world's progress and enlightenment, and the people are lulled in false security,—then, as the midnight thief steals within the unguarded dwelling, so shall sudden destruction come upon the careless and ungodly, "and they shall not escape." *1 Thessalonians 5:2-5.*

Fierce Wasting Tempests

When Jesus revealed to His disciples the fate of Jerusalem and the scenes of the second advent, He foretold also the experience of His people from the time when He should be taken from them, to His return in power and glory for their deliverance. From Olivet the Saviour beheld the storms about to fall upon the apostolic church; and, penetrating deeper into the future, His eye discerned the fierce, wasting tempests that were to beat upon His followers in the coming ages of darkness and persecution. In a few brief utterances of awful significance, He foretold the portion which the rulers of this world would mete out to the church of God. *Matthew 24:9, 21-22.* The followers of Christ must tread the same path of humiliation, reproach, and suffering, which their Master trod. The enmity that burst forth against the world's Redeemer would be manifested against all who should believe on His name.

The history of the early church testified to the fulfillment of the Saviour's words. The powers of earth and hell arrayed themselves against Christ in the person of His followers. Paganism foresaw that should the gospel triumph, her temples and altars would be swept away; therefore she summoned her forces to destroy Christianity. The fires of persecution were kindled. Christians were stripped of their possessions, and driven from their homes. They "endured a great fight of afflictions." *Hebrews 10:32*. They "had trial of cruel mockings and scourgings, yea, moreover of bonds and imprisonment." *Hebrews 11:36*. Great numbers sealed their testimony with their blood. Noble and slave, rich and poor, learned and ignorant, were alike slain without mercy.

Blood Is Seed

Under the fiercest persecution, these witnesses for Jesus kept their faith unsullied. A voice came down to them from the throne of God, "Be thou faithful unto death, and I will give thee a crown of life." *Revelation 2:10*. In vain were Satan's efforts to destroy the church of Christ by violence. The great controversy in which the disciples of Jesus yielded up their lives did not cease when these faithful standard bearers fell at their post. By defeat they conquered. God's workmen were slain, but His work went steadily forward. The gospel continued to spread, and the number of its adherents to increase. It penetrated into regions that were inaccessible, even to the eagles of Rome. Said a Christian, expostulating with the heathen rulers who were urging forward the persecution: "You may torment, afflict, and vex us. Your wickedness puts our weakness to the test, but your cruelty is of no avail. It is but a stronger invitation to bring others to our persuasion. The more we are mowed down, the more we spring up again. The blood of the Christians is seed."

Thousands were imprisoned and slain; but others sprung up to fill their places. And those who were martyred for their faith were secured to Christ, and accounted of Him as conquerors. They had fought the good fight, and they were to receive the crown of glory when Christ should come. The sufferings which they endured brought Christians nearer to one another and to their Redeemer. Their living example and dying testimony were a constant witness for the truth; and, where least expected, the subjects of Satan were leaving his service and enlisting under the banner of Christ.

Deception instead of Persecution

Satan therefore laid his plans to war more successfully against the government of God, by planting his banner in the Christian church. If the followers of Christ could be deceived, and led to displease God, then their strength, fortitude, and firmness would fail, and they would fall an easy prey.

The great adversary now endeavored to gain by artifice what he had failed to secure by force. Persecution ceased, and in its stead were substituted the dangerous allurements of temporal prosperity and worldly honor. Idolaters were led to receive a part of the Christian faith, while they rejected other essential truths. They professed to accept Jesus as the Son of God, and to believe in His death and resurrection; but they had no conviction of sin, and felt no need of repentance or of a change of heart. With some concessions on their part, they proposed that Christians should make concessions, that all might unite on the platform of belief in Christ.

Fearful Peril

Now the church was in fearful peril. Prison, torture, fire, and sword were blessings in comparison with this. Some of the Christians stood firm, declaring that they could make no compromise. Others were in favor of yielding or modifying some features of their faith, and uniting with those who had accepted a part of Christianity, urging that this might be the means of their full conversion. That was a time of deep anguish to the faithful followers of Christ. Under a cloak of pretended Christianity, Satan was insinuating himself into the church, to corrupt their faith and turn their minds from the Word of truth.

Most of the Christians at last consented to lower their standard, and a union was formed between Christianity and paganism. Although the worshipers of idols professed to be converted, and united with the church, they still clung to their idolatry, only changing the objects of their worship to images of Jesus, and even of Mary and the saints. The foul leaven of idolatry, thus brought into the church, continued its baleful work. Unsound doctrines, superstitious rites, and idolatrous ceremonies were incorporated into her faith and worship. As the followers of Christ united with idolaters, the Christian religion became corrupted, and the church lost her purity and power. There were some, however, who were not misled by these delusions. They still maintained their fidelity to the Author of truth, and worshiped God alone.

Desperate Struggle

It required a desperate struggle for those who would be faithful to stand firm against the deceptions and abominations which were disguised in sacerdotal garments and introduced into the church. The Bible was not accepted as the standard of faith. The doctrine of religious freedom was termed heresy, and its upholders were hated and proscribed.

After a long and severe conflict, the faithful few decided to dissolve all union with the apostate church if she still refused to free herself from falsehood and idolatry. They saw that separation was an absolute necessity if they would obey the Word of God. They dared not tolerate errors fatal to their own souls, and set an example which would imperil the faith of their children and children's children. To secure peace and unity they were ready to make any concession consistent with fidelity to God; but they felt that even peace would be too dearly purchased at the sacrifice of principle. If unity could be secured only by the compromise of truth and righteousness, then let there be difference, and even war.

The Great Apostasy

The apostle Paul, in his second letter to the Thessalonians, foretold the great apostasy which would result in the establishment of the papal power. He declared that the day of Christ should not come, "except there come a falling away first, and that man of sin be revealed, the son of perdition; who opposeth and exalteth himself above all that is called God, or that is worshipped; so that he as God sitteth in the temple of God, showing himself that he is God." *2 Thessalonians 2:3-4*. And furthermore, the apostle warns his brethren that "the mystery of iniquity doth already work."

2 Thessalonians 2:7. Even at that early date he saw, creeping into the church, errors that would prepare the way for the development of the papacy.

Little by little, at first in stealth and silence, and then more openly as it increased in strength and gained control of the minds of men, the mystery of iniquity carried forward its deceptive and blasphemous work. Almost imperceptibly the customs of heathenism found their way into the Christian church. The spirit of compromise and conformity was restrained for a time by the fierce persecutions which the church endured under paganism. But as persecution ceased, and Christianity entered the courts and palaces of kings, she laid aside the humble simplicity of Christ and His apostles for the pomp and pride of pagan priests and rulers; and in place of the requirements of God, she substituted human theories and traditions. The nominal conversion of Constantine, in the early part of the fourth century, caused great rejoicing; and the world, cloaked with a form of righteousness, walked into the church. Now the work of corruption rapidly progressed. Paganism, while appearing to be vanquished, became the conqueror. Her spirit controlled the church. Her doctrines, ceremonies, and superstitions were incorporated into the faith and worship of the professed followers of Christ.

The Man of Sin

This compromise between paganism and Christianity resulted in the development of the "man of sin" foretold in prophecy as opposing and exalting himself above God. That gigantic system of false religion is a masterpiece of Satan's power,—a monument of his efforts to seat himself upon the throne to rule the earth according to his will.

Change Times and Laws

The detector of error having been removed, Satan worked according to his will. Prophecy had declared that the papacy was to "think to change times and laws." *Daniel 7:25*. This work it was not slow to attempt. To afford converts from heathenism a substitute for the worship of idols, and thus to promote their nominal acceptance of Christianity, the adoration of images and relics was gradually introduced into the Christian worship. The decree of a general council (Second Council of Nice, A.D. 787) finally established this system of idolatry. To complete the sacrilegious work, Rome presumed to expunge from the law of God the second commandment, forbidding image worship, and to divide the tenth commandment, in order to preserve the number.

The spirit of concession to paganism opened the way for a still further disregard of Heaven's authority. Satan tampered with the fourth Commandment also, and essayed to set aside the ancient Sabbath, the day which God had blessed and sanctified (*Genesis 2:2-3*), and in its stead to exalt the festival observed by the heathen as "the venerable day of the sun." This change was not at first attempted openly. In the first centuries the true Sabbath had been kept by all Christians. They were jealous for the honor of God, and, believing that His law is immutable, they zealously guarded the sacredness of its precepts. But with great subtlety, Satan worked through his agents to bring about his object. That the attention of the people might be called to the Sunday, it was made a festival in honor of the resurrection of Christ. Religious services were held upon it; yet it was regarded as a day of recreation, the Sabbath being still sacredly observed.

To prepare the way for the work which he designed to accomplish, Satan had led the Jews, before the advent of Christ, to load down the Sabbath with the most rigorous exactions, making its observance a burden. Now, taking advantage of the false light in which he had thus caused it to be regarded, he cast contempt upon it as a Jewish institution. While Christians continued to observe the Sunday as a joyous festival, he led them, in order to show their hatred of Judaism, to make the Sabbath a fast, a day of sadness and gloom.

The Day of the Sun

In the early part of the fourth century, the emperor Constantine issued a decree making Sunday a public festival throughout the Roman Empire. The day of the sun was reverenced by his pagan subjects, and was honored by Christians; it was the emperor's policy to unite the conflicting interests of heathenism and Christianity. He was urged to do this by the bishops of the church, who, inspired by ambition and thirst for power, perceived that if the same day was observed by both Christians and the heathen, it would promote the nominal acceptance of Christianity by pagans, and thus advance the power and glory of the church. But while Christians were gradually led to regard Sunday as possessing a degree of sacredness, they still held the true Sabbath as the holy of the Lord, and observed it in obedience to the fourth commandment.

The Commandments of Men

The arch-deceiver had not completed his work. He was resolved to gather the Christian world under his banner, and to exercise his power through his vicegerent, the proud pontiff who claimed to be the representative of Christ. Through half-converted pagans, ambitious prelates, and world-loving churchmen, he accomplished his purpose. Vast councils were held from time to time, in which the dignitaries of the church were convened from all the world. In nearly every council the Sabbath which God had instituted was pressed down a little lower, while the Sunday was correspondingly exalted. Thus the pagan festival came finally to be honored as a divine institution while the Bible Sabbath was pronounced a relic of Judaism, and its observers were declared to be accursed.

The great apostate had succeeded in exalting himself "above all that is called God, or that is worshiped." *2 Thessalonians 2:4.* He had dared to change the only precept of the divine law that unmistakably points all mankind to the true and living God. In the fourth commandment, God is revealed as the Creator of the heavens and the earth, and is thereby distinguished from all false gods. It was as a memorial of the work of creation that the seventh day was sanctified as a rest day for man. It was designed to keep the living God ever before the minds of men as the source of being and the object of reverence and worship. Satan strives to turn men from their allegiance to God and from rendering obedience to His law; therefore he directs his efforts especially against that commandment which points to God as the Creator.

Child of the Papacy

Protestants now urge that the resurrection of Christ on Sunday made it the Christian Sabbath. But Scripture evidence is lacking. No such honor was given to the day by Christ or his apostles. The observance of Sunday as a Christian institution had its origin in that "mystery of lawlessness." *2 Thessalonians 2:7, R. V.*, which even in Paul's day, had begun its work. Where and when did the Lord adopt this child of the papacy? What valid reason can be given for a change which the Scriptures do not sanction?

Papal Supremacy

In the sixth century the papacy had become firmly established. Its seat of power was fixed in the imperial city, and the bishop of Rome was declared to be the head over the entire church. Paganism had given place to the papacy. The dragon had given to the beast "his power, and his seat, and great authority." *Revelation 13:2*. And now began the 1260 years of papal oppression foretold in the prophecies of Daniel and the Revelation. *Daniel 7:25; Revelation 13:5-7*. Christians were forced to choose, either to yield their integrity and accept the papal ceremonies and worship or to wear away their lives in dungeons or suffer death by the rack, the fagot, or the headsman's ax. Now were fulfilled the words of Jesus, "Ye shall be betrayed both by parents, and brethren, and kinsfolks, and friends; and some of you shall they cause to be put to death. And ye shall be hated of all men for my name's sake." *Luke 21:16-17*. Persecution opened upon the faithful with greater fury than ever before, and the world became a vast battlefield. For hundreds of years the church of Christ found refuge in seclusion and obscurity. Thus says the prophet: "The woman fled into the wilderness, where she hath a place prepared of God, that they should feed her there a thousand two hundred and threescore days." *Revelation 12:6*.

The Dark Ages

The accession of the Roman Church to power marked the beginning of the Dark Ages. As her power increased, the darkness deepened. Faith was transferred from Christ, the true foundation, to the pope of Rome. Instead of trusting in the Son of God for forgiveness of sins and for eternal salvation, the people looked to the pope and to the priests and prelates to whom he delegated authority. They were taught that the pope was their earthly mediator, and that none could approach God except through him; and, further, that he stood in the place of God to them, and was therefore to be implicitly obeyed. A deviation from his requirements was sufficient cause for the severest punishment to be visited upon the bodies and souls of the offenders. Thus the minds of the people were turned away from God to fallible, erring, and cruel men; nay more, to the prince of darkness himself, who exercised his power through them. Sin was disguised in a garb of sanctity. When the Scriptures are suppressed, and man comes to regard himself as supreme, we need look only for fraud, deception, and debasing iniquity. With the elevation of human laws and traditions was manifest the corruption that ever results from setting aside the law of God.

Flight into the Wilderness

Among the leading causes that had led to the separation of the true church from Rome was the hatred of the latter toward the Bible Sabbath. As foretold by prophecy, the papal power cast down the truth to the ground. The law of God was trampled in the dust, while the traditions and customs of men were exalted. The churches that were under the rule of the papacy were early compelled to honor the Sunday as a holy day. Amid the prevailing error and superstition, many, even of the true people of God, became so bewildered that while they observed the Sabbath they refrained from labor also on the Sunday. But this did not satisfy the papal leaders. They demanded not only that Sunday be hallowed, but that the Sabbath be profaned; and they denounced in the strongest language those who dared to show it honor. It was only by fleeing from the power of Rome that any could obey

God's law in peace.

In Lands Beyond

In lands beyond the jurisdiction of Rome, there existed for many centuries bodies of Christians who remained almost wholly free from papal corruption. They were surrounded by heathenism, and in the lapse of ages were affected by its errors; but they continued to regard the Bible as the only rule of faith, and adhered to many of its truths. These Christians believed in the perpetuity of the law of God, and observed the Sabbath of the fourth commandment. Churches that held to this faith and practice existed in Central Africa and among the Armenians of Asia.

The Waldenses

But of those who resisted the encroachments of the papal power, the Waldenses stood foremost. In the very land where popery had fixed its seat, there its falsehood and corruption were most steadfastly resisted . . The persecutions visited for many centuries upon this God-fearing people were endured by them with a patience and constancy that honored their Redeemer. Notwithstanding the crusades against them, and the inhuman butchery to which they were subjected, they continued to send out their missionaries to scatter the precious truth. They were hunted to the death; yet their blood watered the seed sown, and it failed not of yielding fruit. Thus the Waldenses witnessed for God, centuries before the birth of Luther. Scattered over many lands, they planted the seeds of the Reformation that began in the time of Wycliffe, grew broad and deep in the days of Luther, and is to be carried forward to the close of time by those who also are willing to suffer all things for "the Word of God, and for the testimony of Jesus Christ." *Revelation 1:9.*

The Reformation Continues

The reformation did not, as many suppose, end with Luther. It is to be continued to the close of this world's history. Luther had a great work to do in reflecting to others the light which God had permitted to shine upon him; yet he did not receive all the light which was to be given to the world. From that time to this, new light has been continually shining upon the Scriptures, and new truths have been constantly unfolding.

Bridging the Chasm

The English reformers, while renouncing the doctrines of Romanism, had retained many of its forms. Thus though the authority and the creed of Rome were rejected, not a few of her customs and ceremonies were incorporated into the worship of the Church of England. It was claimed that these things were not matters of conscience, that though they were not commanded in Scripture, and hence were nonessential, yet not being forbidden, they were not intrinsically evil. Their observance tended to narrow the gulf which separated the reformed churches from Rome, and it was urged that they would promote the acceptance of the Protestant faith by Romanists. To the conservative and compromising, these arguments seemed conclusive. But there was another class that did not so judge. The fact that these customs tended to bridge the chasm between Rome and the Reformation, was in their view a conclusive argument against retaining them. They looked upon them as badges of the slavery from which they had been delivered, and to which they had no disposition to return. They reasoned that God has in His Word established the regulations governing His worship, and that men are not at liberty to add to these or to detract from them. The very beginning of the great apostasy was in seeking to supplement the authority of God by that of the church. Rome began by enjoining what God had not forbidden, and she ended by forbidding what He had explicitly enjoined.

Sealing the Law

The work of Sabbath reform to be accomplished in the last days is foretold in the prophecy of Isaiah: "Thus saith the Lord, Keep ye judgment, and do justice: for my salvation is near to come, and my righteousness to be revealed. Blessed is the man that doeth this, and the son of man that layeth hold on it; that keepeth the Sabbath from polluting it, and keepeth his hand from doing any evil." "The sons of the stranger, that join themselves to the Lord, . . to be His servants, every one that keepeth the Sabbath from polluting it, and taketh hold of My covenant; even them will I bring to My holy mountain, and make them joyful in My house of prayer." *Isaiah 56:1, 2, 6, 7.*

These words apply in the Christian age, as is shown by the context: "The Lord God which gathereth the outcasts of Israel saith, Yet will I gather others to him, beside those that are gathered unto him." *Isaiah 56:8.* Here is foreshadowed the gathering in of the Gentiles by the gospel. And upon those who then honor the Sabbath, a blessing is pronounced. Thus the obligation of the fourth commandment extends past the crucifixion, resurrection, and ascension of Christ, to the time when His servants should preach to all nations the message of glad tidings.

The Lord commands by the same prophet, "Bind up the testimony, seal the law among My disciples." *Isaiah 8:16.* The seal of God's law is found in the fourth commandment. This only, of all the ten, brings to view both the name and the title of the Lawgiver. It declares him to be the Creator of the heavens and the earth, and thus shows His claim to reverence and worship above all others. Aside from this precept, there is nothing in the decalogue to show by whose authority the law is given. When the Sabbath was changed by the papal power, the seal was taken from the law. The disciples of Jesus are called upon to restore it, by exalting the Sabbath of the fourth commandment to its rightful position as the Creator's memorial and the sign of His authority.

"To the law and to the testimony." While conflicting doctrines and theories abound, the law of God is the one unerring rule by which all opinions, doctrines, and theories are to be tested. Says the prophet, "If they speak not according to this word, it is because there is no light in them." *Isaiah 8:20.*

The prophet thus points out the ordinance which has been forsaken: "Thou shalt raise up the foundations of many generations; and thou shalt be called, The repairer of the breach, The restorer of paths to dwell in. If thou turn away thy foot from the Sabbath, from doing thy pleasure on My holy day; and call the Sabbath a delight, the holy of the Lord, honorable; and shalt honor Him, not doing thine own ways, nor finding thine own pleasure, nor speaking thine own words; then shalt thou delight thyself in the Lord." *Isaiah 58:12-14.* This prophecy also applies in our time. The breach was made in the law of God when the Sabbath was changed by the Roman power. But the time has come for that divine institution to be restored. The breach is to be repaired, and the foundation of many generations to be raised up.

Hallowed by the Creator's rest and blessing, the Sabbath was kept by Adam in his innocence in holy Eden; by Adam, fallen yet repentant, when he was driven from his happy estate. It was kept by all the patriarchs, from Abel to righteous Noah, to Abraham, to Jacob. When the chosen people were in bondage in Egypt, many, in the midst of prevailing idolatry, lost their knowledge of God's law; but when the Lord delivered Israel, He proclaimed His law in awful grandeur to the assembled multitude, that they might know His will, and fear and obey Him forever.

From that day to the present, the knowledge of God's law has been preserved in the earth, and the Sabbath of the fourth commandment has been kept. Though the "man of sin" succeeded in trampling under foot God's holy day, yet even in the period of his supremacy there were, hidden in secret places, faithful souls who paid it honor. Since the Reformation, there have been some in every generation to maintain its observance. Though often in the midst of reproach and persecution, a constant testimony has been borne to the perpetuity of the law of God and the sacred obligation of the creation Sabbath.

Truth Is Older than Error

Many urged that Sunday-keeping had been an established doctrine and a widespread custom of the church for many centuries. Against this argument it was shown that the Sabbath and its observance were more ancient and widespread, even as old as the world itself, and bearing the sanction both of angels and of God. When the foundations of the earth were laid, when the morning stars sang together, and all the sons of God shouted for joy, then was laid the foundation of the Sabbath (*Job 38:6-7; Genesis 2:1-3*). Well may this institution demand our reverence: it was ordained by no human authority, and rests upon no human traditions; it was established by the Ancient of days, and commanded by His eternal Word.

Six days shalt thou labour and do all thy work:
But the seventh day is the Sabbath
Of the Lord thy God.
In it thou shalt not do any work . .
For in six days the Lord made heaven and earth,
The sea, and all that in them is,
And rested the seventh day.
Wherefore the Lord blessed the Sabbath day, and hallowed it.
— The Fourth Commandment (Exodus 20:9-11)

There was war in heaven, . . and Satan
Was cast out into the earth . .
And the dragon . . went to make war
With the remnant of her seed,
Which keep the commandments of God,
And have the testimony of Jesus Christ.
— Revelation 12:7, 9, 17

He that hath the Son
hath life;
And he that hath not the Son of God
hath not life.
—1 John 5:12

Except ye eat the flesh of the Son of man,
And drink His blood, ye have no life in you.
— John 6:53

I am the way, the truth, and the life.
— John 14:6

CHAPTER SIXTEEN

The Crisis in Our Time

A woman married a man who did not love her, a man whom she found to be very cruel. Life seemed to be but a round of drudgery to her.

And all his demands!

He wanted her to get up every morning at 5 a.m. sharp, cook his breakfast, then serve it promptly at 6—and on and on. She had to wait on him continually, and he was very exacting in his demands on her time. She felt miserable trying to do all that he asked. And so the years rolled by.

Finally her husband died, and after a few years she remarried. This time she married a very kindly man; they loved each other deeply.

The months turned into years; and then one day, while clearing out some old papers in the attic, she came across the strict set of rules that her first husband had written out for her to obey.

Carefully she read through them,—and with surprise discovered that she was now following every one of them! "Getup at five. Serve breakfast at six sharp." On and on she read. She was doing it all! And why?

Because now she loved her husband and he loved her! Following the rules, because of love, had become a happy task.

And so it is with obedience to God. He has given us a wonderful set of rules to guide our lives. Only the One who made us can know the best guidelines for our lives. God's moral law for mankind is the Ten Commandments (Exodus 20:3-17).

That Law comes from One who deeply loves us. In those ten brief statements are to be found the Standard of purity and right living for all of God's children.

As we consider the Law of God, we can be thankful for such a loving Father in heaven who gave it to us. Such a law is an expression of how deep His love for us is. And, in addition, He has in His Written Word given us health and sanitary laws as well. In nature and in our bodies we find physical laws that must be obeyed.

When we view this obedience as but a means of expressing our thankfulness—and showing our love in return,—then we enter upon a higher sphere of living. Indeed, we are living as do the angels in heaven. For they find their happiness in serving and obeying God continually. They love to do it. And because they do it, they are happy.

In heaven, obedience to God and love to God go together. If, in your heart, you find that you would rather not obey God—or, that perhaps you think that you need not obey Him,—then I suggest that if you will come alone to Him in prayer, and plead for a new heart and a deeper surrender,—that He can and will give you the answers you need. It is the love of God that constrains us—urges us, enables us,—to obey all that He has asked of us. And as we yield our lives in obedience to His Written Word, He is preparing us for an eternal life in heaven.

For up there everyone will love and obey Him through the ceaseless ages of eternity. Christ died on Calvary to enable each one of us—through His overcoming grace—to obey Him and become like Him.

Those who had accepted the light concerning the mediation of Christ and the perpetuity of the law of God, found that these were the truths presented in Revelation 14. The messages of this chapter constitute a threefold warning, which is to prepare the inhabitants of the earth for the Lord's second coming.

The Hour of His Judgment

The announcement, "The hour of His Judgment is come," points to the closing work of Christ's ministration for the salvation of men. It heralds a truth which must be proclaimed until the Saviour's intercession shall cease, and He shall return to the earth to take His people to Himself. The work of judgment, which began in 1844, must continue until the cases of all are decided, both of the living and the dead; hence it will extend to the close of human probation. That men may be prepared to stand in the Judgment, the message commands them to "fear God, and give glory to Him," "and worship Him that made heaven, and earth, and the sea, and the fountains of waters." The result of an acceptance of these messages is given in the words, "Here are they that keep the commandments of God, and the faith of Jesus."

In order to be prepared for the Judgment, it is necessary that men should keep the law of God. That law will be the standard of character in the Judgment. The apostle Paul declares, "As many as have sinned in the law shall be judged by the law; . . in the day when God shall judge the secrets of men by Jesus Christ." And he says that "the doers of the law shall be justified." *Rom. 2:12-16.* Faith is essential in order to keep of the law of God; for "without faith it is impossible to please Him." And "whatsoever is not of faith is sin." *Heb. 11:6; Rom. 14:23.*

By the first angel, men are called upon to "fear God, and give glory to Him," and to worship Him as the Creator of the heavens and the earth. In order to do this, they must obey His law. Says the wise man, "Fear God, and keep His commandments; for this is the whole duty of man." *Eccl. 12:13.* Without obedience to His commandments, no worship can be pleasing to God. "This is the love of God, that we keep His commandments." "He that turneth away his ear from hearing the law, even his prayer shall be abomination." *1 John 5:3; Prov. 28:9.*

Worship the Creator

The duty to worship God is based upon the fact that He is the Creator, and that to Him all other beings owe their existence. And wherever, in the Bible, His claim to reverence and worship above the gods of the heathen is presented, there is cited the evidence of His creative power. "All the gods of the nations are idols; but the Lord made the heavens." *Ps. 96:5.* "To whom then will ye liken me, or shall I be equal? saith the Holy One. Lift up your eyes on high, and behold who hath created these things." "Thus saith the Lord that created the heavens; God Himself that formed the earth and made it; . . I am the Lord; and there is none else." *Isa. 40:25-26; 45:18.* Says the Psalmist: "Know ye that the Lord, He is God: it is He that hath made us, and not we ourselves." "O come, let us worship and bow down: let us kneel before the Lord our Maker." *Ps. 100:3; 95:6.* And the holy beings who worship God in Heaven state, as the reason why their homage is due to Him, "Thou art worthy, O Lord, to receive glory and honor and power: for Thou hast created all things." Revelation 4:11.

In Revelation 14, men are called upon to worship the Creator, and the prophecy brings to view a class that, as the result of the threefold message, are keeping the commandments of God. One of these commandments points directly to God as the Creator. The fourth precept declares: "The seventh day is the Sabbath of the Lord thy God . . For in six days the Lord made heaven and earth, the sea, and all that in them is, and rested the seventh day; wherefore the Lord blessed the Sabbath day, and hallowed it." *Ex. 20:10-11.* Concerning the Sabbath, the Lord says further: that it is "a sign, . . that ye may know that I am the Lord your God." Eze. 20:20. And the reason given is, "For in six days the Lord made heaven and earth, and on the seventh day He rested, and was refreshed." *Ex. 31:17.*

Sabbath - Worship - Creator

"The importance of the Sabbath as the memorial of creation is that it keeps ever present the true reason why worship is due to God,"—because He is the Creator and we His creatures. "The Sabbath therefore lies at the very foundation of divine worship; for it teaches this great truth in the most impressive manner, and no other institution does this. The true ground of divine worship, not of that on the seventh day merely, but of all worship, is found in the distinction between the Creator and His creatures. This great fact can never become obsolete, and must never be forgotten." It was to keep this truth ever before the minds of men that God instituted the Sabbath in Eden; and so long as the fact that He is our Creator continues to be a reason why we should worship Him, so long the Sabbath will continue as its sign and memorial. Had the Sabbath been universally kept, man's thoughts and affections would have been led to the Creator as the object of reverence and worship, and there would never have been an idolater, an atheist, or an infidel. The keeping of the Sabbath is a sign of loyalty to the true God, "Him that made heaven and earth, and the sea, and the fountains of waters." It follows that the message which commands men to worship God and keep His commandments, will especially call upon them to keep the fourth commandment.

If Any Man Worship the Beast

In contrast to those who keep the commandments of God and have the faith of Jesus, the third angel points to another class, against whose errors a solemn and fearful warning is uttered: "If any man worship the beast and his image, and receive his mark in his forehead, or in his hand, the same shall drink of the wine of the wrath of God." *Rev. 14:9-10.* A correct interpretation of the symbols employed is necessary to an understanding of this message. What is represented by the beast, the image, the mark?

The line of prophecy in which these symbols are found begins with Revelation 12, with the dragon that sought to destroy Christ at His birth. The dragon is said to be Satan (Rev. 12:9); he it was that moved upon Herod to put the

Saviour to death. But the chief agent of Satan in making war upon Christ and His people during the first centuries of the Christian era was the Roman Empire, in which paganism was the prevailing religion. Thus, while the dragon primarily represents Satan, it is, in a secondary sense, a symbol of pagan Rome.

The Beast of Revelation 13

In Chapter 13 (verses 1-10) is described another beast, "like unto a leopard," to which the dragon gave "his power, and his seat, and great authority." This symbol, as most Protestants have believed, represents the papacy, which succeeded to the power and seat and authority once possessed by the ancient Roman Empire. Of the leopard-like beast it is declared: "There was given unto him a mouth speaking great things and blasphemies. And he opened his mouth in blasphemy against God, to blaspheme His name, and His tabernacle, and them that dwell in Heaven. And it was given unto him to make war with the saints, and to overcome them; and power was given him over all kindreds, and tongues, and nations." *Rev. 13:15-17.* This prophecy, which is nearly identical with the description of the little horn of Daniel 7, unquestionably points to the papacy.

Forty and Two Months

"Power was given unto him to continue forty and two months." And, says the prophet, "I saw one of his heads as it were wounded to death." And again. "He that leadeth into captivity shall go into captivity; he that killeth with the sword must be killed with the sword." The forty and two months are the same as the "time and times and the dividing of time," three years and a half, or 1260 days, of Daniel 7,—the time during which the papal power was to oppress God's people. This period, as stated in preceding chapters, began with the establishment of the papacy, A.D. 538, and terminated in 1798. At that time, when the papacy was abolished and the pope made captive by the French army, the papal power received its deadly wound, and the prediction was fulfilled, "He that leadeth into captivity shall go into captivity."

Lamb-like Beast

At this point another symbol is introduced. Says the prophet, "I beheld another beast coming up out of the earth; and he had two horns like a lamb." *Rev. 13:11.* Both the appearance of this beast and the manner of its rise indicate that the nation which it represents is unlike those presented under the preceding symbols. The great kingdoms that have ruled the world were presented to the prophet Daniel as beasts of prey, rising when the "four winds of the heaven strove upon the great sea." *Dan. 7:2.* In Revelation 17, an angel explained that waters represent "peoples, and multitudes, and nations, and tongues." *Rev. 17:15.* Winds are a symbol of strife. The four winds of heaven striving upon the great sea, represent the terrible scenes of conquest and revolution by which kingdoms have attained to power.

Out of the Earth

But the beast with the lamb-like horns was seen "coming up out of the earth." Instead of overthrowing other powers to establish itself, the nation thus represented must arise in territory previously unoccupied, and grow up gradually and peacefully. It could not, then, arise among the crowded and struggling nationalities of the Old World,—that turbulent sea of "peoples, and multitudes, and nations, and tongues." It must be sought in the Western Continent.

What nation of the New World was in 1798 rising into power, giving promise of strength and greatness, and attracting the attention of the world? The application of the symbol admits of no question. One nation, and only one, meets the specifications of this prophecy; it points unmistakably to the United States of America. Again and again the thought, almost the exact words, of the sacred writer have been unconsciously employed by the orator and the historian in describing the rise and growth of this nation. The beast was seen "coming up out of the earth"; and, according to the translators, the word here rendered "coming up" literally signifies to "grow or spring up as a plant." And, as we have seen, the nation must arise in territory previously unoccupied. A prominent writer—describing the rise of the United States—

speaks of "the mystery of her coming forth from vacancy," and says, "Like a silent seed we grew into empire" (Townsend, in *The New World Compared with the Old, p. 462*). A European journal in 1850 spoke of the United States as a wonderful empire, which was "emerging," and "amid the silence of the earth daily adding to its power and pride." (*The Dublin Nation*) Edward Everett, in an oration on the Pilgrim founders of this nation, said: "Did they look for a retired spot, inoffensive from its obscurity, safe in its remoteness from the haunts of despots, where the little church of Leyden might enjoy freedom of conscience? Behold the mighty regions over which, in peaceful conquest, . . they have borne the banners of the cross."

Like a Lamb

"And he had two horns like a lamb." The lamb-like horns indicate youth, innocence, and gentleness, fitly representing the character of the United States when presented to the prophet as "coming up" in 1798. The Christian exiles who first fled to America sought an asylum from royal oppression and priestly intolerance, and they determined to establish a government upon the broad foundation of civil and religious liberty. The Declaration of Independence sets forth the great truth that "all men are created equal," and endowed with the inalienable right to "life, liberty, and the pursuit of happiness." And the Constitution guarantees to the people the right of self-government, providing that representatives elected by the popular vote shall enact and administer the laws. Freedom of religious faith was also granted, every man being permitted to worship God according to the dictates of his conscience. Republicanism and Protestantism became the fundamental principles of the nation. These principles are the secret of its power and prosperity. The oppressed and down-trodden throughout Christendom have turned to this land with interest and hope. Millions have sought its shores, and the United States has risen to a place among the most powerful nations of the earth.

Spake as a Dragon

But the beast with lamb-like horns and dragon voice of

the symbol point to a striking contradiction between the professions and the practice of the nation thus represented. The "speaking" of the nation is the action of its legislative and judicial authorities. By such action it will give the lie to those liberal and peaceful principles which it has put forth as the foundation of its policy. The prediction that it will speak "as a dragon," and exercise "all the power of the first beast," plainly foretells a development of the spirit of intolerance and persecution that was manifested by the nations represented by the dragon and the leopard-like beast. And the statement that the beast with two horns "causeth the earth and them which dwell therein to worship the first beast," indicates that the authority of this nation is to be exercised in enforcing some observance which shall be an act of homage to the papacy.

Such action would be directly contrary to the principles of this government, to the genius of its free institutions, to the direct and solemn avowals of the Declaration of Independence, and to the Constitution. The founders of the nation wisely sought to guard against the employment of the secular power on the part of the church, with its inevitable result—intolerance and persecution. The Constitution provides that "Congress shall make no law respecting an establishment of religion, or prohibiting the free exercise thereof," and that "no religious test shall ever be required as a qualification to any office of public trust under the United States." Only in flagrant violation of these safeguards to the nation's liberty can any religious observance be enforced by civil authority. But the inconsistency of such action is no greater than is represented in the symbol. It is the beast with lamb-like horns—in profession pure, gentle, and harmless—that speaks as a dragon.

Make an Image

"Saying to them that dwell on the earth, that *they* should make an image to the beast." Here is clearly presented a form of government in which the legislative power rests with the people; a most striking evidence that the United States is the nation denoted in the prophecy.

But what is the "image to the beast"? and how is it to be formed? The image is made by the two-horned beast, and is an image *to* the first beast. Then to learn what the image is like, and how it is to be formed, we must study the characteristics of the beast itself,—the papacy. When the early church became corrupted by departing from the simplicity of the gospel, and accepting heathen rites and customs, she lost the Spirit and power of God; and in order to control the consciences of the people, she sought the support of the secular power. The result was the papacy, a church that controlled the power of the State, and employed it to further her own ends, especially for the punishment of "heresy." In order for the United States to form an image to the beast, the religious power must so control the civil government that the authority of the State will also be employed by the church to accomplish her own ends.

Whenever the church has obtained secular power, she has employed it to punish dissent from her doctrines. Apostasy in the church will prepare the way for the image to the beast.

When the leading churches of the United States, uniting upon such points of doctrine as are held by them in common, shall influence the State to enforce their decrees and to sustain their institutions, then Protestant America will have formed an image of the Roman hierarchy, and the infliction of civil penalties upon dissenters will inevitably result.

The Third Angel's Warning

The beast with two horns "causeth [commands] all, both small and great, rich and poor, free and bond, to receive a mark in their right hand, or in their foreheads: and that no man might buy or sell, save he that had the mark, or the name of the beast, or the number of his name." *Rev. 13:16-17.* The third angel's warning is, "If any man worship the beast and his image, and receive his mark in his forehead, or in his hand, the same shall drink of the wine of the wrath of God." "The beast" mentioned in this message, whose worship is enforced by the two-horned beast, is the first, or leopard-like beast of Revelation 13,—the papacy. The "image to the beast" represents that form of apostate Protestantism which will be developed when the Protestant churches shall seek the aid of the civil power for the enforcement of their dogmas. The "mark of the beast" still remains to be defined.

After the warning against the worship of the beast and his image, the prophecy declares, "Here are they that keep the commandments of God, and the faith of Jesus." Since those who keep God's commandments are thus placed in contrast with those that worship the beast and his image and receive his mark, it follows that the keeping of God's law, on the one hand, and its violation, on the other, will make the distinction between the worshipers of God and the worshipers of the beast.

Think to Change

The special characteristic of the beast, and therefore of his image, is the breaking of God's commandments. Says Daniel of the little horn, the papacy, "He shall think to change the times and the law." *Dan. 7:25, R.V.* And Paul styled the same power the "man of sin," who was to exalt himself above God. One prophecy is a complement of the other. Only by changing God's law could the papacy exalt itself above God; whoever should understandingly keep the law as thus changed would be giving supreme honor to that power by which the change was made. Such an act of obedience to papal laws would be a mark of allegiance to the pope in the place of God.

The papacy has attempted to change the law of God. The second commandment, forbidding image worship, has been dropped from the law, and the fourth commandment has been so changed as to authorize the observance of the first instead of the seventh day as the Sabbath. But papists urge, as a reason for omitting the second commandment, that it is unnecessary, being included in the first, and that they are giving the law exactly as God designed it to be understood. This cannot be the change foretold by the prophet. An intentional, deliberate change is presented: "He shall *think* to change the times and the law." The change in the fourth commandment exactly fulfills the prophecy. For this, the only authority claimed is that of the church. Here the papal power openly sets itself above God.

The Bible or the Papacy

While the worshipers of God will be especially distinguished by their regard for the fourth commandment,—since this is the sign of His creative power and the witness to His claim upon man's reverence and homage,—the worshipers of the beast will be distinguished by their efforts to tear down the Creator's memorial, to exalt the institution of Rome. It was in behalf of the Sunday that popery first asserted its arrogant claims; and its first resort to the power of the State was to compel the observance of Sunday as "the Lord's day." But the Bible points to the seventh day, and not to the first, as the Lord's day. Said Christ, "The Son of man is Lord also of the Sabbath." The fourth commandment declares, "The seventh day is the Sabbath of the Lord." And by the prophet Isaiah the Lord designates it, "My holy day." *Mark 2:28; Isa. 58:13.*

The claim so often put forth, that Christ changed the Sabbath, is disproved by His own words. It is a fact generally admitted by Protestants, that the Scriptures give no authority for the change of the Sabbath. Roman Catholics acknowledge that the change of the Sabbath was made by their church, and declare that Protestants, by observing the Sunday, are recognizing her power.

The Mark of Papal Authority

As the sign of the authority of the Catholic Church, papist writers cite "the very act of changing the Sabbath into Sunday, which Protestants allow of . . because by keeping Sunday strictly they acknowledge the church's power to ordain feasts, and to command them under sin." (*Abridgement of Christian Doctrine, p. 58, H. Tuberville.*) What then is the change of the Sabbath, but the sign or mark of the authority of the Romish Church—"the mark of the beast?"

The Roman Church has not relinquished her claim to supremacy; and when the world and the Protestant churches accept a sabbath of her creating—while they reject the Bible Sabbath—they virtually admit this assumption. They may claim the authority of tradition and of the Fathers for the change; but in so doing they ignore the very principle which separates them from Rome,—that "the Bible, and the Bible only, is the religion of Protestants." The papists can see that they are deceiving themselves, willingly closing their eyes to the facts in the case. As the movement for Sunday enforcement gains favor, he rejoices, feeling assured that it will eventually bring the whole Protestant world under the banner of Rome.

Worshiping the Beast

Romanists declare that "the observance of Sunday by the Protestants is an homage they pay, in spite of themselves, to the authority of the [Catholic] Church" (*"Plain Talk about Protestantism," p. 213*). The enforcement of Sunday-keeping on the part of Protestant churches is an enforcement of the worship of the papacy—of the beast. Those who, understanding the claims of the fourth commandment, choose to observe the false instead of the true Sabbath, are thereby paying homage to that power by which alone it is commanded. But in the very act of enforcing a religious duty by secular power, the churches would themselves form an image to the beast; hence the enforcement of Sunday-keeping in the United States would be an enforcement of the worship of the beast and his image.

But Christians of past generations observed the Sunday, supposing that in so doing they were keeping the Bible Sabbath; and there are now true Christians in every church, not excepting the Roman Catholic communion, who honestly believe that Sunday is the Sabbath of divine appointment. God accepts their sincerity of purpose and their integrity before Him. But when Sunday observance shall be enforced by law, and the world shall be enlightened concerning the obligation of the true Sabbath, then whoever shall transgress the command of God, to obey a precept which has no higher authority than that of Rome, will thereby honor popery above God. He is paying homage to Rome, and to the power which enforces the institution ordained by Rome. He is worshiping the beast and his image. As men then reject the institution which God has declared to be the sign of His authority, and honor in its stead that which Rome has chosen as the token of her supremacy, they will thereby accept the sign of allegiance to Rome—"the mark of the beast." And it is not until the issue is thus plainly set before the people—and they are brought to choose between the commandments of God and the commandments of men—that those who continue in transgression will receive "the mark of the beast."

The Warning Against the Mark

The most fearful threatening ever addressed to mortals is contained in the third angel's message. That must be a terrible sin which calls down the wrath of God unmingled with mercy. Men are not to be left in darkness concerning this important matter; the warning against this sin is to be given to the world before the visitation of God's judgments, that all may know why they are to be inflicted, and have opportunity to escape them. Prophecy declares that the first angel would make his announcement to "every nation, and kindred, and tongue, and people." The warning of the third angel, which forms a part of the same threefold message, is to be no less widespread. It is represented in the prophecy as proclaimed with a loud voice, by an angel flying in the midst of heaven; and it will command the attention of the world!

Two Great Classes

In the issue of the contest, all Christendom will be divided into two great classes,—those who keep the commandments of God and the faith of Jesus, and those who worship the beast and his image and receive his mark. Although church and State will unite their power to compel "all, both small and great, rich and poor, free and bond, to receive "the mark of the beast" (*Rev. 13:16*), yet the people of God will not receive it. The prophet of Patmos beholds "them that had gotten the victory over the beast, and over his image, and over his mark, and over the number of his name stand on the sea of glass, having the harps of God," and singing the song of Moses and the Lamb. *Revelation 15:2-3.*

Protestants Are Changing

Romanism is now regarded by Protestants with far

greater favor than in former years. In those countries where Catholicism is not in the ascendancy, and the papists are taking a conciliatory course in order to gain influence, there is an increasing indifference concerning the doctrines that separate the reformed churches from the papal hierarchy; the opinion is gaining ground that, after all, we do not differ so widely upon vital points as has been supposed, and that a little concession on our part will bring us into a better understanding with Rome. The time was when Protestants placed a high value upon the liberty of conscience which has been so dearly purchased. They taught their children to abhor popery, and held that to seek harmony with Rome would be disloyalty to God. But how widely different are the sentiments now expressed. The defenders of popery declare that the church has been maligned; and the Protestant world are inclined to accept the statement. Many urge that it is unjust to judge the church of today by the abominations and absurdities that marked her reign during the centuries of ignorance and darkness. They excuse her horrible cruelty as the result of the barbarism of the times, and plead that the influence of modern civilization has changed her sentiments.

Babylon Has Not Changed

Have these persons forgotten the claim of infallibility put forth for nine hundred years by this haughty power? So far from being relinquished, this claim has been affirmed in the twentieth century with greater positiveness than ever before. As Rome asserts that she *"never erred, and never can err,"* how can she renounce the principles which governed her course in past ages?

The papal church will never relinquish her claim to infallibility. All that she has done in her persecution of those who reject her dogmas, she holds to be right; and would she not repeat the same acts, should the opportunity be presented? Let the restraints now imposed by secular governments be removed, and Rome be reinstated in her former power, and there would speedily be a revival of her tyranny and persecution.

Forgetting the Past

The Roman Church now presents a fair front to the world, covering with apologies her record of horrible cruelties. She has clothed herself in Christ-like garments; but she is unchanged. Every principle of popery that existed in past ages exists today. The doctrines devised in the darkest ages *are still held.* Let none deceive themselves. The popery that Protestants are now so ready to honor is the same that ruled the world in the days of the Reformation, when men of God stood up, at the peril of their lives, to expose her iniquity. She possesses the same pride and arrogant assumption that lorded it over kings and princes, and claimed the prerogatives of God. Her spirit is no less cruel and despotic now than when she crushed out human liberty and slew the saints of the Most High.

The papacy is just what prophecy declared that she would be, the apostasy of the latter times (*2 Thess. 2:3-4*). It is a part of her policy to assume the character which will best accomplish her purpose; but beneath the variable appearance of the chameleon, she conceals the invariable venom of the serpent. "We are not bound to keep faith and promises to heretics," she declares. Shall this power, whose record for a thousand years is written in the blood of the saints, be now acknowledged as a part of the church of Christ?

What Has Changed

It is not without reason that the claim has been put forth in Protestant countries, that Catholicism differs less widely from Protestantism than in former times. There has been a change; but the change is not in the papacy. Catholicism indeed resembles much of the Protestantism that now exists, because Protestantism has so greatly degenerated since the days of the reformers

A prayerful study of the Bible would show Protestants the real character of the papacy, and would cause them to abhor and to shun it; but many are so wise in their own conceit that they feel no need of humbly seeking God that they may be led into the truth. Although priding themselves on their enlightenment, they are ignorant both of the Scriptures and of the power of God. They must have some means of quieting their consciences; and they seek that which is least spiritual and humiliating. *What they desire is a method of forgetting God which shall pass as a method of remembering Him.* The papacy is well adapted to meet the wants of all these. It is prepared for two classes of mankind, embracing nearly the whole world,—those who would be saved by their merits, and those who would be saved in their sins. Here is the secret of its power.

A day of great intellectual darkness has been shown to be favorable to the success of popery. It will yet be demonstrated that a day of great intellectual light is equally favorable for its success.

Following in the Steps

In the movements now in progress in the United States to secure for the institutions and usages of the church the support of the state, Protestants are following in the steps of papists. Nay, more, they are opening the door for the papacy to regain in Protestant America the supremacy which she has lost in the Old World. And that which gives greater significance to this movement is the fact that the principal object contemplated is the enforcement of Sunday observance,—a custom which originated with Rome, and which she claims as the sign of her authority. It is the spirit of the papacy—the spirit of conformity to worldly customs, the veneration for human traditions above the commandments of God,—that is permeating the Protestant churches, and leading them on to do the same work of Sunday exaltation which the papacy has done before them.

These records of the past clearly reveal the enmity of Rome toward the true Sabbath and its defenders, and the means which she employs to honor the institution of her creating.

Protestants little know what they are doing when they propose to accept the aid of Rome in the work of Sunday exaltation. While they are bent upon the accomplishment of their purpose, Rome is aiming to re-establish her power, to recover her lost supremacy. Let history testify of her artful and persistent efforts to insinuate herself into the affairs of nations; and having gained a foothold, to further her own aims, even at the ruin of princes and people. Romanism openly puts forth the claim that the pope "can pronounce sentences and judgments in contradiction to the right of nations, to the law of God and man" (the *"Decretalia"*).

And let it be remembered: it is the boast of Rome that she never changes. The principles of Gregory VII and Innocent III are still the principles of the Roman Church. And had she but the power, she would put them in practice with as much vigor now as in past centuries. Let the principle once be established in the United States, that the church may employ or control the power of the State; that religious observances may be enforced by secular laws; in short, that the authority of church and State is to dominate the conscience—and the triumph of Rome in this country is assured.

Bind up the testimony, seal the law
among My disciples.
— Isaiah 8:16

But I would not have you
To be ignorant, brethren,
Concerning them which are asleep,
That ye sorrow not,
Even as others which have no hope.
— I Thessalonians 4:13

And many of them that sleep
In the dust of the earth shall awake.
— Daniel 12:2

For the Lord Himself shall descend from heaven, . .
And the dead in Christ shall rise first.
— I Thessalonians 4:16

CHAPTER SEVENTEEN

A Masterpiece of Deception

A widowed woman had but one child, a son, whom she raised. Over the years, they had a deep companionship, and when he was drafted into the army, it was with sorrow that they said good-bye to one another.

Soon letters began coming regularly from her boy. However, when he was shipped overseas to the front lines, the letters came less often.

Eventually they stopped entirely.

One day an army officer came to her home with the news that her son was missing in action. The shock was almost more than she could take. She cried and cried, but her tears could not be quenched.

Close friends told her that Christ could solve her problems, but she decided in her heart that she needed her son more than she needed Christ.

Just then, a different neighbor stopped by her home. He said that the spirits had told him that she was ready to see her son, and that he had come to invite her down the street to his seance parlor. "Come tonight," he said. Christian friends advised her not to go, and showed her what it says in the Bible about spiritualism (Isaiah 8:19-

20; Leviticus 19:31; 1 Chronicles 10:13-14; Malachi 3:5; Deuteronomy 18:10-13; 13:1-4; Exodus 22:18; Leviticus 20:27, Galatians 5:20-23; Revelation 16:14; 1 Timothy 4:1; 2 Corinthians 11:14-15; Matthew 24:23-24; 1 Peter 5:8). And they warned her that the spirits would lie to her (Jeremiah 27:9-10; 2 Thessalonians 2:9-10).

Hesitating, she thought about it for several days. But feeling that the Bible meant less to her than the hope of seeing her son at the seance parlor, she went.

Seated in a dark room that smelled as if it had never seen sunlight, she watched as the medium muttered strange things as he appeared to look intently at something she could not see.

Then something that looked exactly like her son appeared before her! He wore the same army uniform she last saw him in, and coming quickly to her, hugged her to him. Sitting on a couch together they recalled events of years gone by.

Night after night, she returned to the seance parlor, and the two would sit together on the couch, hug and kiss, and share memories of the past. He also began telling her new ways to live her life.

Friends noticed that the mother seemed to lose her interest in religious things, and stopped attending church. But since she would take no counsel in the matter, for six months all they could do was pray.

Then one day her boy came home. Of course, it seemed unbelievable—but for her especially so! Unknown to the government, he had been in an enemy prison camp, and while there knew that he would never come out alive. But then, unexpectedly, he was released.

The lying spirits in the seance parlor saw her no more. For she never returned.

To this day she thanks God for bringing her boy back—and delivering her from a bondage to the spirits and eternal death.

With the earliest history of man, Satan began his efforts to deceive our race. He who had incited rebellion in Heaven desired to bring the inhabitants of the earth to unite with him in his warfare against the government of God. Adam and Eve had been perfectly happy in obedience to the law of God, and this fact was a constant testimony against the claim which Satan had urged in Heaven, that God's law was oppressive, and opposed to the good of His creatures. And, furthermore, Satan's envy was excited as he looked upon the beautiful home prepared for the sinless pair. He determined to cause their fall, that having separated them from God, and brought them under his own power, he might gain possession of the earth, and here establish his kingdom, in opposition to the Most High.

"The woman said unto the serpent, We may eat of the fruit of the trees of the garden: but of the fruit of the tree which is in the midst of the garden God hath said, Ye shall not eat of it, neither shall ye touch it, lest ye die. And the serpent said unto the woman, Ye shall not surely die; for God doth know that in the day ye eat thereof, then your eyes shall be opened, and ye shall be as gods, knowing good and evil." *Gen. 3:2-5.*

Immortality by Obedience

In the midst of Eden grew the tree of life, whose fruit had the power of perpetuating life. Had Adam remained obedient to God, he would have continued to enjoy free access to this tree, and would have lived forever. But when he sinned, he was cut off from partaking of the tree of life, and he became subject to death. The divine sentence, "Dust thou art, and unto dust shalt thou return," points to the utter extinction of life.

Immortality, promised to man on condition of obedience, had been forfeited by transgression. Adam could not transmit to his posterity that which he did not possess; and there could have been no hope for the fallen race, had not God—by the sacrifice of His Son—"brought life and immortality to light through the gospel." *Rom. 5:12; 2 Tim. 1:10.* And only through Christ can immortality be obtained.

Said Jesus, "He that believeth on the Son hath everlasting life; and he that believeth not the Son shall not see life." *John 3:36*. Every man may come in possession of this priceless blessing if he will comply with the conditions. All "who by patient continuance in well-doing seek for glory and honor and immortality," will receive eternal life (*Rom. 2:7*).

No Immortal Sinner

The only one who promised Adam life in disobedience was the great deceiver. And the declaration of the serpent to Eve in Eden,—"Ye shall not surely die,"—was the first sermon ever preached upon the immortality of the soul. Yet this declaration, resting solely upon the authority of Satan, is echoed from the pulpits of Christendom, and is received by the majority of mankind as readily as it was received by our first parents. The divine sentence, "The soul that sinneth, it shall die" (*Ezek. 18:20*) is made to mean, The soul that sinneth, it shall not die, but live eternally. We cannot but wonder at the strange infatuation which renders men so credulous concerning the words of Satan, and so unbelieving in regard to the words of God.

Had man, after his fall, been allowed free access to the tree of life, he would have lived forever, and thus sin would have been immortalized. But cherubim and a flaming sword kept "the way of the tree of life" (*Gen. 3:24*), and not one of the family of Adam has been permitted to pass that barrier and partake of the life-giving fruit. Therefore there is not an immortal sinner.

"Ye Shall Not Surely Die"

But after the fall, Satan bade his angels make a special effort to inculcate the belief in man's natural immortality; and having induced the people to receive this error, they were to lead them on to conclude that the sinner would live in eternal misery. Now the prince of darkness, working through his agents, represents God as a revengeful tyrant, declaring that he plunges into hell all those who do not please Him, and causes them ever to feel His wrath; and that while they suffer unutterable anguish and writhe in the eternal flames, their Creator looks down upon them with satisfaction.

Misrepresenting God's Character

How repugnant to every emotion of love and mercy, and even to our sense of justice, is the doctrine that the wicked dead are tormented with fire and brimstone in an eternally burning hell; that for the sins of a brief, earthly life they are to suffer torture as long as God shall live. Yet this doctrine has been widely taught, and is still embodied in many of the creeds of Christendom. It is urged that the infliction of endless misery upon the wicked would show God's hatred of sin as an evil which is ruinous to the peace and order of the universe. Oh, dreadful blasphemy! As if God's hatred of sin is the reason why He perpetuates sin. For, according to the teachings of these theologians, continued torture without hope of mercy maddens its wretched victims, and as they pour out their rage in curses and blasphemy, they are forever augmenting their load of guilt. God's glory is not enhanced by thus perpetuating continually increasing sin through ceaseless ages.

The Opposite Error

A large class to whom the doctrine of eternal torment is revolting are driven to the opposite error. They see that the Scriptures represent God as a being of love and compassion, and they cannot believe that He will consign His creatures to the fires of an eternally burning hell. But, holding that the soul is naturally immortal, they see no alternative but to conclude that all mankind will finally be saved. Many regard the threatenings of the Bible as designed merely to frighten men into obedience, and not to be literally fulfilled. Thus the sinner can live in selfish pleasure, disregarding the requirements of God, and yet expect to be finally received into His favor. Such a doctrine, presuming upon God's mercy—but ignoring His justice—pleases the carnal heart, and emboldens the wicked in their iniquity.

The Wages of Sin Is Death

God has given in His Word decisive evidence that He will punish the transgressors of His law. Those who flatter themselves, that He is too merciful to execute justice upon the sinner, have only to look to the cross of Calvary. The death of the spotless Son of God testifies that "the wages of sin is death," that every violation of God's law must receive its just retribution. Christ the sinless became sin for man. He bore the guilt of transgression, and the hiding of His Father's face, until His heart was broken and His life crushed out. All this sacrifice was made that sinners might be redeemed. In no other way could man be freed from the penalty of sin. And every soul that refuses to become a partaker of the atonement provided at such a cost must bear, in his own person, the guilt and punishment of transgression.

"He that overcometh shall inherit all things; and I will be his God, and he shall be My son." *Rev. 21:7*. Here, also, conditions are specified. In order to inherit all things, we must resist and overcome sin.

Obedience by Faith in Christ

"No fornicator, nor unclean person, nor covetous man, who is an idolater, hath any inheritance in the kingdom of Christ and God." *Eph. 5:5, R.V.* "Follow peace with all men, and holiness, without which no man shall see the Lord." *Heb. 12:14*. "Blessed are they that do His commandments, that they may have right to the tree of life, and may enter in through the gates into the city. For without are dogs, and sorcerers, and whoremongers, and murderers, and idolaters, and whosoever loveth and maketh a lie." *Rev. 22:14-15*.

For the Good of All

God executes justice upon the wicked, for the good of the universe, and even for the good of those upon whom His judgments are visited. He would make them happy if He could do so in accordance with the laws of His government and the justice of His character. He surrounds them with the tokens of His love, He grants them a knowledge of His law, and follows them with the offers of His mercy; but they despise His love, make void His law, and reject His mercy.

Those who have chosen Satan as their leader, and have been controlled by his power, are not prepared to enter the presence of God. Pride, deception, licentiousness, and cruelty have become fixed in their characters. Can they enter Heaven, to dwell forever with those whom they despised and hated on earth? Truth will never be agreeable to a liar; meekness will not satisfy self-esteem and pride; purity is not acceptable to the corrupt; disinterested love does not appear attractive to the selfish. What source of enjoyment could Heaven offer to those who are wholly absorbed in earthly and selfish interests?

Life or Death

"The wages of sin is death; but the gift of God is eternal life through Jesus Christ our Lord." *Rom. 6:23.* While life is the inheritance of the righteous, death is the portion of the wicked. Moses declared to Israel: "I have set before thee this day life and good, and death and evil." *Deut. 30:15.* The death referred to in these scriptures is not that pronounced upon Adam, for all mankind suffer the penalty of his transgression. It is the "second death" that is placed in contrast with everlasting life.

In consequence of Adam's sin, death passed upon the whole human race. All alike go down into the grave. And through the provisions of the plan of salvation, all are to be brought forth from their graves. "There shall be a resurrection of the dead, both of the just and unjust;" *Acts 24:15.* "For as in Adam all die, even so in Christ shall all be made alive." *1 Cor. 15:22.*

But a distinction is made between the two classes that are brought forth. "All that are in the graves shall hear His voice, and shall come forth; they that have done good, unto the resurrection of life; and they that have done evil, unto the resurrection of damnation." *John 5:28-29.* They who have been "accounted worthy" of the resurrection of life are "blessed and holy." "On such the second death hath no power." *Rev. 20:6.* But those who have not through repentance and faith secured pardon, must receive the penalty of transgression,—"the wages of sin." They suffer punishment varying in duration and intensity, "according to their works," but finally ending in the second death.

Since it is impossible for God, consistently with His justice and mercy to save the sinner in his sins, He deprives him of the existence which his transgressions have forfeited, and of which he has proved himself unworthy. Says an inspired writer, "Yet a little while, and the wicked shall not be; yea, thou shalt diligently consider his place, and it shall not be." And another declares, "They shall be as though they had not been." *Ps. 37:10; Obad. 16*. Covered with infamy, they sink into hopeless, eternal oblivion.

An End of Sin

Thus will be made an end of sin, with all the woe and ruin which have resulted from it. Says the psalmist: "Thou hast destroyed the wicked, Thou hast put out their name forever and ever. O thou enemy, destructions are come to a perpetual end." *Ps. 9:5-6*. John, in the Revelation, looking forward to the eternal state, hears a universal anthem of praise undisturbed by one note of discord. Every creature in Heaven and earth was heard ascribing glory to God (*Rev. 5:13*). There will then be no lost souls to blaspheme God, as they writhe in never-ending torment; no wretched beings in hell will mingle their shrieks with the songs of the saved.

A Second Error

Upon the fundamental error of natural immortality rests the doctrine of consciousness in death—a doctrine, like eternal torment, opposed to the teachings of the Scriptures, to the dictates of reason, and to our feelings of humanity. According to the popular belief, the redeemed in Heaven are acquainted with all that takes place on the earth, and especially with the lives of the friends whom they have left behind. But how could it be a source of happiness to the dead to know the troubles of the living, to witness the sins committed by their own loved ones, and to see them enduring all the sorrows, disappointments, and anguish of life? How much of Heaven's bliss would be enjoyed by those who were hovering over their friends on earth? And how utterly revolting is the belief that as soon as the breath leaves the body, the soul of the impenitent is consigned to the flames of hell! To what depths of anguish must those be plunged who see their friends passing to the grave unprepared, to enter upon an eternity of woe and sin! Many have been driven to insanity by this harrowing thought.

The Bible Says

What say the Scriptures concerning these things? David declares that man is not conscious in death. "His breath goeth forth, he returneth to his earth; in that very day his thoughts perish." *Ps. 146:4*. Solomon bears the same testimony: "The living know that they shall die; but the dead know not anything." "Their love, and their hatred, and their envy, is now perished; neither have they any more a portion forever in anything that is done under the sun." "There is no work, nor device, nor knowledge, nor wisdom, in the grave, whither thou goest." *Eccl. 9:5, 6, 10.*

When, in answer to his prayer, Hezekiah's life was prolonged fifteen years, the grateful king rendered to God a tribute of praise for His great mercy. In this song he tells the reason why he thus rejoices: "The grave cannot praise Thee, death cannot celebrate Thee; they that go down into the pit cannot hope for Thy truth. The living, the living, he shall praise Thee, as I do this day." *Isa. 38:18-19*. Popular theology represents the righteous dead as in Heaven, entered into bliss, and praising God with an immortal tongue; but Hezekiah could see no such glorious prospect in death. With his words agrees the testimony of the psalmist: "In death there is no remembrance of Thee; in the grave who shall give Thee thanks?" "The dead praise not the Lord, neither any that go down into silence." *Ps. 6:5; 115:17.*

And said Paul: "If the dead rise not, then is not Christ raised: and if Christ be not raised, your faith is vain; ye are yet in your sins. Then they also which are fallen asleep in Christ are perished." *1 Corinthians 15:16-18.* If for four thousand years the righteous had gone directly to Heaven at death, how could Paul have said that if there is no resurrection, "they which are fallen asleep in Christ are perished?" No resurrection would be necessary.

The Truth of the Resurrection

It is an undeniable fact that the hope of immortal blessedness at death has led to widespread neglect of the Bible doctrine of the resurrection. But when about to leave His disciples, Jesus did not tell them that they would soon come to Him. "I go to prepare a place for you," He said. "And if I go and prepare a place for you, I will come again, and receive you unto Myself." *John 14:2-3.* And Paul tells us, further, that "the Lord Himself shall descend from Heaven with a shout, with the voice of the archangel, and with the trump of God; and the dead in Christ shall rise first. Then we which are alive and remain shall be caught up together with them in the clouds to meet the Lord in the air: and so shall we ever be with the Lord." And he adds, "Comfort one another with these words." *1 Thess. 4:16-18.*

Paul points his brethren to the future coming of the Lord, when the fetters of the tomb shall be broken and the "dead in Christ" shall be raised to eternal life.

The Investigative Judgment

Before any can enter the mansions of the blest, their cases must be investigated, and their characters and their deeds must pass in review before God. All are to be judged according to the things written in the books, and to be rewarded as their works have been. This Judgment does not take place at death. Mark the words of Paul: "He hath appointed a day, in the which He will judge the world in righteousness by that man whom He hath ordained; whereof He hath given assurance unto all men, in that He hath raised Him from the dead." *Acts 17:31.* Here the apostle plainly stated that a specified time, then future, had been fixed upon for the Judgment of the world. Jude refers to the same period (*Jude 14-15*), and so does John in the Revelation (*Rev. 20:12*). But if the dead are already enjoying the bliss of Heaven or writhing in the flames of hell, what need of a future Judgment? The teachings of God's Word on these important points are neither obscure nor contradictory; they may be understood by common minds. But what candid mind can see either wisdom or justice in the current theory?

Glorious Awakening

The Bible clearly teaches that the dead do not go immediately to Heaven. They are represented as sleeping until the resurrection (*1 Thess. 4:14; Job 14:10-12*). In the very day when the silver cord is loosed and the golden bowl broken (*Eccl. 12:6*), man's thoughts perish. They that go down to the grave are in silence. They know no more of anything that is done under the sun (*Job 14:21*).

Blessed rest for the weary righteous! Time, be it long or short, is but a moment to them. They sleep, they are awakened by the trump of God to a glorious immortality. "For the trumpet shall sound, and the dead shall be raised incorruptible . . So when this corruptible shall have put on incorruption, and this mortal shall have put on immortality, then shall be brought to pass the saying that is written, Death is swallowed up in victory." *1 Cor. 15:52-54*. As they are called forth from their deep slumber, they begin to think just where they ceased. The last sensation was the pang of death, the last thought that they were falling beneath the power of the grave. When they arise from the tomb, their first glad thought will be echoed in the triumphal shout, "O death, where is thy sting? O grave, where is thy victory?" *1 Cor. 15:55*.

Preparation for Spiritualism

The doctrine of man's consciousness in death, especially the belief that the spirits of the dead return to minister to the living, has prepared the way for modern Spiritualism. Here is a channel regarded as sacred, through which Satan works for the accomplishment of his purposes. The fallen angels who do his bidding appear as messengers from the spirit world. While professing to bring the living into communication with the dead, the prince of evil exercises his bewitching influence upon their minds.

Satanic Counterfeits

He has power to bring before men the appearance of their departed friends. The counterfeit is perfect; the familiar look, the words, the tone are reproduced with marvelous distinctness. Many are comforted with the assurance that their loved ones are enjoying the bliss of Heaven; and without suspicion of danger, they give ear to "seducing spirits, and doctrines of devils."

When they have been led to believe that the dead actually return to communicate with them, Satan causes those to appear who went into the grave unprepared. They claim to be happy in Heaven, and even to occupy exalted positions there; and thus the error is widely taught, that no difference is made between the righteous and the wicked. The pretended visitants from the world of spirits sometimes utter cautions and warnings which prove to be correct. Then, as confidence is gained, they present doctrines that directly undermine faith in the Scriptures.

A Supernatural Power

Many will be ensnared through the belief that Spiritualism is a merely human imposture; when brought face to face with manifestations which they cannot but regard as supernatural, they will be deceived, and will be led to accept them as the great power of God.

These persons overlook the testimony of the Scriptures concerning the wonders wrought by Satan and his agents. It was by satanic aid that Pharaoh's magicians were enabled to counterfeit the work of God. Paul testifies that before the second advent of Christ there will be similar manifestations of satanic power. The coming of the Lord is to be preceded by "the working of Satan with all power and signs and lying wonders, and with all deceivableness of unrighteousness." *2 Thess. 2:9-10.* No mere impostures are here foretold. Men are deceived by the miracles which Satan's agents have power to do, not which they pretend to do.

Something for Everyone

The prince of darkness, who has so long bent the powers of his mastermind to the work of deception, skillfully adapts his temptations to men of all classes and conditions. To persons of culture and refinement he presents Spiritualism in its more refined and intellectual aspects, and thus succeeds in drawing many into his snare.

Satan beguiles men now as he beguiled Eve in Eden, by flattery, by kindling a desire to obtain forbidden knowledge, by exciting ambition for self-exaltation. It was cherishing these evils that caused his fall, and through them he aims to compass the ruin of men. "Ye shall be as gods," he declares, "knowing good and evil." *Gen. 3:5.* Thus, in place of the righteousness and perfection of the infinite God, the true object of adoration—in place of the perfect righteousness of His law, the true standard of human attainment—Satan has substituted the sinful, erring nature of man himself as the only object of adoration, the only rule of judgment, or standard of character. This is progress, not upward, but downward.

To the self-indulgent, the pleasure-loving, the sensual, Spiritualism presents itself under a less subtle disguise than to the more refined and intellectual; in its grosser forms they find that which is in harmony with their inclinations. When the people are thus led to believe that desire is the highest law, that liberty is license, and that man is accountable only to himself, who can wonder that corruption and depravity teem on every hand? Multitudes eagerly accept teachings that leave them at liberty to obey the promptings of the carnal heart.

None Need Be Deceived

But none need be deceived by the lying claims of Spiritualism. God has given the world sufficient light to enable them to discover the snare. As already shown, the theory which forms the very foundation of Spiritualism is at war with the plainest statements of Scripture. The Bible declares that the dead know not anything, that their thoughts have perished; they have no part in anything that is done under the sun; they know nothing of the joys or sorrows of those who were dearest to them on earth.

Furthermore, God has expressly forbidden all pretended communication with departed spirits. In the days of the Hebrews there was a class of people who claimed—as do the Spiritualists of today—to hold communication with the dead. But the "familiar spirits" (as these visitants from other worlds were called), are declared by the Bible to be the "spirits of devils." (Compare Num. 25:1-3; Ps. 106:28; 1 Cor. 10:20; Rev. 16:14.) The work of dealing with familiar spirits was pronounced an abomination to the Lord, and was solemnly forbidden under penalty of death (*Lev. 19:31; 20:27*).

The very name of witchcraft is now held in contempt. The claim that men can hold intercourse with evil spirits is regarded as a fable of the Dark Ages. But Spiritualism, which numbers its converts by hundreds of thousands, yea, by millions—which has made its way into scientific circles, which has invaded churches, and has found favor in legislative bodies, and even in the courts of kings—this mammoth deception is but a revival, in a new guise, of the witchcraft condemned and prohibited of old. If there were no other evidence of the real character of Spiritualism, it should be enough for the Christian that the spirits make no difference between righteousness and sin, between the noblest and purest of the apostles of Christ and the most corrupt of the servants of Satan.

A Terrible Power

There are few who have any just conception of the deceptive power of Spiritualism and the danger of coming under its influence. Many tamper with it merely to gratify their curiosity. They have no real faith in it, and would be filled with horror at the thought of yielding themselves to the spirits' control. But they venture upon the forbidden ground, and the mighty destroyer exercises his power upon them against their will. Let them once be induced to submit their minds to his direction, and he holds them captive. It is impossible in their own strength to break away from the bewitching, alluring spell. Nothing but the power of God, granted in answer to the earnest prayer of faith, can deliver these ensnared souls.

Delusion by Choice

Says the prophet Isaiah: "When they shall say unto you, Seek unto them that have familiar spirits, and unto wizards that peep, and that mutter: should not a people seek unto their God? for the living to the dead? To the law and to the testimony: if they speak not according to this word, it is because there is no light in them." *Isa. 8:19-20*. If men had been willing to receive the truth so plainly stated in the Scriptures concerning the nature of man and the state of the dead, they would see in the claims and manifestations of Spiritualism the working of Satan with power and signs and lying wonders. But rather than yield the liberty so agreeable to the carnal heart and renounce the sins which they love, multitudes close their eyes to the light and walk straight on, regardless of warnings while Satan weaves his snares about them, and they become his prey. "Because they received not the love of the truth, that they might he saved"; therefore "God shall send them strong delusion, that they should believe a lie." *2 Thess. 2:10-11*. Those who would stand in this time of peril must understand for themselves the testimony of the Scriptures.

Know Your Bible

Many will be confronted by the spirits of devils personating beloved relatives or friends, and declaring the most dangerous heresies. These visitants will appeal to our tenderest sympathies, and will work miracles to sustain their pretensions. We must be prepared to withstand them with the Bible truth that the dead know not anything, and that they who thus appear are the spirits of devils.

The Hour of Temptation

Just before us is the "hour of temptation, which shall come upon all the world, to try them that dwell upon the earth." *Rev. 3:10*. All whose faith is not firmly established upon the Word of God will be deceived and overcome. Satan "works with all deceivableness of unrighteousness" to gain control of the children of men; and his deceptions will continually increase. But he can gain his object only as men voluntarily yield to his temptations. Those who are earnestly seeking a knowledge of the truth, and are striving to purify their souls through obedience, thus doing what they can to prepare for the conflict will find, in the God of truth, a sure defense. "Because thou hast kept the word of My patience, I also will keep thee" (*Rev. 3:10*), is the Saviour's promise. He would sooner send every angel out of Heaven to protect His people, than leave one soul that trusts in Him to be overcome by Satan.

A Covenant with Death

The prophet Isaiah brings to view the fearful deception which will come upon the wicked, causing them to count themselves secure from the judgments of God: "We have made a covenant with death, and with hell are we at agreement; when the overflowing scourge shall pass through, it shall not come unto us; for we have made lies our refuge, and under falsehood have we hid ourselves." *Isa. 28:15.*

Satan's Masterpiece

Satan has long been preparing for his final effort to deceive the world. The foundation of his work was laid by the assurance given to Eve in Eden, "Ye shall not surely die." "In the day ye eat thereof, then your eyes shall be opened, and ye shall be as gods, knowing good and evil." *Gen. 3:4-5.* Little by little he has prepared the way for his masterpiece of deception in the development of Spiritualism. He has not yet reached the full accomplishment of his designs; but it will be reached in the last remnant of time. Says the prophet: "I saw three unclean spirits like frogs; . . they are the spirits of devils, working miracles, which go forth unto the kings of the earth and of the whole world, to gather them to the battle of that great day of God Almighty." *Rev. 16:13-14.* Except those who are kept by the power of God through faith in His Word, the whole world will be swept into the ranks of this delusion. The people are fast being lulled to a fatal security, to be awakened only by the outpouring of the wrath of God.

Saith the Lord God: "Judgment also will I lay to the line, and righteousness to the plummet; and the hail shall sweep away the refuge of lies, and the waters shall overflow the hiding place. And your covenant with death shall be disannulled, and your agreement with hell shall not stand; when the overflowing scourge shall pass through, then ye shall be trodden down by it." *Isa. 28:17-18.*

The wages of sin is death. —Romans 6:23.
For the living know that they shall die. But the dead know not any thing. —Ecclesiastes 9:5.
His breath goeth forth, He returneth to his earth; In that very day his thoughts perish. —Psalm 146:4.
For in death There is no remembrance of Thee. —Psalm 6:5.

CHAPTER EIGHTEEN

Entering the Final Crisis

There is a crisis coming on this earth. Thinking men everywhere recognize it. But few understand its exact nature; yet the God of heaven in His written Word has given man warning of what is coming on this earth and what must be done to meet it.

More and more the world is setting at naught the claims of God. Men have become bold in transgression. The wickedness of the inhabitants of the world has almost filled up the measure of their iniquity. The substitution of the laws of men for the law of God is the last act in the drama.

Men in their blindness boast of wonderful progress and enlightenment, but the heavenly watchers see the earth filled with corruption and violence. We are living in the midst of an epidemic of crime, at which thoughtful, God-fearing men everywhere are aghast. The spirit of anarchy is permeating all nations, and the outbreaks of strife and bloodshed are but indications of what is ahead.

We are standing on the threshold of the crisis of the ages. In quick succession judgments are following one another. The restraining Spirit of God is even now

being withdrawn from the world. Hurricanes, storms, tempests, fire and flood, disasters by sea and land are to be seen. Science seeks to explain all these. The signs thickening around us—warning of the end and of Christ's coming in judgment—are attributed to any other than the true cause.

The sun shines in the sky, passing over its usual round, and the heavens still declare the glory of God. Men are still eating and drinking, planting and building, marrying and giving in marriage. Merchants are still buying and selling. Men are jostling one against another, contending for the highest place. Pleasure lovers are still crowding to horse races, gambling halls, theaters, and worldly music,—even bringing it all into their homes. The highest excitement prevails, yet probation's hour is fast closing and every case is about to be eternally decided.

Satan sees that his time is short. He has set all his agencies at work that men may be deceived, deluded, occupied, and entranced until the day of probation shall be ended and the door of mercy forever shut.

We are on the verge of great and solemn events. Prophecies are fulfilling. Strange events are taking place. Everything in our world is in agitation.

The final crisis is stealing gradually upon us. Transgression—rebellion against the law of God—has almost reached its limit. Confusion fills the world, and a great terror is soon to come upon human beings. The end is very near. We must seek God and cling to the Bible and His Ten Commandments. We must prepare for what is soon to break upon the world as an overwhelming surprise.

In this time of prevailing iniquity we may know that the last great crisis is at hand. When the defiance of God's law is almost universal, when His people are oppressed and afflicted by their fellow men, the Lord will interpose.

—from the writings of E.G. White, slightly adapted.

From the very beginning of the great controversy in Heaven it has been Satan's purpose to overthrow the law of God. It was to accomplish this that he entered upon his rebellion against the Creator; and though he was cast out of Heaven, he has continued the same warfare upon the earth. To deceive men, and thus lead them to transgress God's law, is the object which he has steadfastly pursued. Whether this be accomplished by casting aside the law altogether or by rejecting one of its precepts, the result will be ultimately the same. He that offends "in one point," manifests contempt for the whole law; his influence and example are on the side of transgression; he becomes "guilty of all." *James 2:10.*

In seeking to cast contempt upon the divine statutes, Satan has perverted the doctrines of the Bible, and errors have thus become incorporated into the faith of thousands who profess to believe the Scriptures. The last great conflict between truth and error is but the final struggle of the long-standing controversy concerning the law of God. Upon this battle we are now entering,—a battle between the laws of men and the precepts of God, between the religion of the Bible and the religion of fable and tradition.

No Error More Bold

No error accepted by the Christian world strikes more boldly against the authority of Heaven, none is more directly opposed to the dictates of reason, none is more pernicious in its results, than the modern doctrine so rapidly gaining ground that God's law is no longer binding upon men. Every nation has its laws, which command respect and obedience; no government could exist without them; and can it be conceived that the Creator of the heavens and the earth has no law to govern the beings he has made? Suppose that prominent ministers were publicly to teach that the statutes which govern their land and protect the rights of its citizens were not obligatory,—that they restricted the liberties of the people, and therefore ought not to be obeyed; how long would such men be tolerated in the pulpit? But is it a graver offense to disregard the laws of States and nations than to trample upon those divine precepts which are the foundation of all government?

It would be far more consistent for nations to abolish their statutes, and permit the people to do as they please, than for the Ruler of the universe to annul His law, and leave the world without a standard to condemn the guilty or justify the obedient. Would we know the result of making void the law of God? The experiment has been tried. Terrible were the scenes enacted in France when atheism became the controlling power. It was then demonstrated to the world that to throw off the restraints which God has imposed is to accept the rule of the cruelest of tyrants. When the standard of righteousness is set aside, the way is open for the prince of evil to establish his power in the earth.

What Lawlessness Will Bring

Wherever the divine precepts are rejected, sin ceases to appear sinful, or righteousness desirable. Those who refuse to submit to the government of God are wholly unfitted to govern themselves. Through their pernicious teachings, the spirit of insubordination is implanted in the hearts of children and youth, who are naturally impatient of control; and a lawless, licentious state of society results. While scoffing at the credulity of those who obey the requirements of God, the multitudes eagerly accept the delusions of Satan. They give the rein to lust, and practice the sins which have called down judgments upon the heathen.

Those who teach the people to lightly regard the commandments of God sow disobedience, to reap disobedience. Let the restraint imposed by the divine law be wholly cast aside, and human laws would soon be disregarded. Because God forbids dishonest practices—coveting, lying, and defrauding—men are ready to trample upon His statutes as a hindrance to their worldly prosperity; but the results of banishing these precepts would be such as they do not anticipate. If the law were not binding, why should any fear to transgress? Property would no longer be safe. Men would obtain their neighbor's possessions by violence; and the strongest would become richest. Life itself would not be respected. The marriage vow would no longer stand as a sacred bulwark to protect the family. He who had the power would, if he desired, take his neighbor's wife by violence. The fifth commandment would be set aside with the fourth. Children would not shrink from taking the life of their parents, if by so doing they could obtain the desire of their corrupt hearts. The civilized world would become a horde of robbers and assassins; and peace, rest, and happiness would be banished from the earth.

And it Is Already Happening

Already the doctrine that men are released from obedience to God's requirements has weakened the force of moral obligation, and opened the floodgates of iniquity upon the world. Lawlessness, dissipation, and corruption are sweeping in upon us like an overwhelming tide. In the family Satan is at work. His banner waves, even in professedly Christian households. There is envy, evil surmising, hypocrisy, estrangement, emulation, strife, betrayal of sacred trusts, indulgence of lust. The whole system of religious principles and doctrines which should form the foundation and framework of social life seems to be a tottering mass, ready to fall to ruin.

The Last Great Delusion

"To the law and to the testimony: If they speak not according to this word, it is because there is no light in them." *Isa. 8:20.* The people of God are directed to the Scriptures as their safe-guard against the influence of false teachers and the delusive power of spirits of darkness. Satan employs every possible device to prevent men from obtaining a knowledge of the Bible; for its plain utterances reveal his deceptions. At every revival of God's work, the prince of evil is aroused to more intense activity; he is now putting forth his utmost efforts for a final struggle against Christ and his followers. The last great delusion is soon to open before us. Antichrist is to perform his marvelous works in our sight. So closely will the counterfeit resemble the true, that it will be impossible to distinguish between them except by the Holy Scriptures. By their testimony every statement and every miracle must be tested.

Those who endeavor to obey all the commandments of God will be opposed and derided. They can stand only in God. In order to endure the trial before them, they must understand the will of God as revealed in His Word; they can honor Him only as they have a right conception of His character, government, and purposes, and act in accordance with them. None but those who have fortified the mind with the truths of the Bible will stand through the last great conflict. To every soul will come the searching test, Shall I obey God rather than men? The decisive hour is even now at hand. Are our feet planted on the rock of God's immutable Word? Are we prepared to stand firm in defense of the commandments of God and the faith of Jesus?

Counterfeit before the Genuine

Before the final visitation of God's judgments upon the earth, there will be, among the people of the Lord, such a revival of primitive godliness as has not been witnessed since apostolic times. The Spirit and power of God will be poured out upon His children. At that time many will separate themselves from those churches in which the love of this world has supplanted love for God and His Word. Many, both of ministers and people, will gladly accept those great truths which God has caused to be proclaimed at this time, to prepare a people for the Lord's second coming. The enemy of souls desires to hinder this work; and before the time for such a movement shall come, he will endeavor to prevent it by introducing a counterfeit. In those churches which he can bring under his deceptive power, he will make it appear that God's special blessing is poured out; there will be manifest what is thought to be great religious interest. Multitudes will exult that God is working marvelously for them, when the work is that of another spirit. Under a religious guise, Satan will seek to extend his influence over the Christian world.

In many of the revivals which have occurred during the last half century, the same influences have been at work, to a greater or less degree, that will be manifest in the more extensive movements of the future. There is an emotional excitement, a mingling of the true with the false, that is well adapted to mislead. Yet none need be deceived. In the light of God's Word it is not difficult to determine the nature of these movements. Wherever men neglect the testimony of the Bible, turning away from those plain, soul-testing truths which require self-denial and renunciation of the world, there we may be sure that God's blessing is not bestowed. And by the rule which Christ Himself has given, "Ye shall know them by their fruits" (*Matt. 7:16*), it is evidence that these movements are not the work of the Spirit of God.

False Revivals and the True

In the truths of His Word, God has given to men a revelation of Himself; and to all who accept them they are a shield against the deceptions of Satan. It is a neglect of these truths that has opened the door to the evils which are now becoming so widespread in the religious world. The nature and the importance of the law of God have been, to a great extent, lost sight of. A wrong conception of the character, the perpetuity, and obligation of the divine law has led to errors in relation to conversion and sanctification, and has resulted in lowering the standard of piety in the church. Here is to be found the secret of the lack of the Spirit and power of God in the revivals of our time.

And then the great deceiver will persuade men that those who serve God are causing these evils. The class that have provoked the displeasure of Heaven will charge all their troubles upon those whose obedience to God's commandments is a perpetual reproof to transgressors. It will be declared that men are offending God by the violation of the Sunday-sabbath, that this sin has brought calamities which will not cease until Sunday observance shall be strictly enforced, and that those who present the claims of the fourth commandment—thus destroying reverence for Sunday—are troublers of the people, preventing their restoration to divine favor and temporal prosperity.

Double Deception

Satan's policy in this final conflict with God's people is the same that he employed in the opening of the great controversy in Heaven. He professed to be seeking to promote the stability of the divine government, while secretly bending every effort to secure its overthrow. And the very work which he was thus endeavoring to accomplish he charged upon the loyal angels. The same policy of deception has marked the history of the Roman Church. It has professed to act as the vicegerent of Heaven while seeking to exalt itself above God and to change His law. While Satan seeks to destroy those who honor God's law, he will cause them to be accused as law-breakers, as men who are dishonoring God and bringing judgments upon the world.

Religious Law, the Key

God never forces the will or the conscience; but Satan's constant resort—to gain control of those whom he cannot otherwise seduce—is compulsion by cruelty. Through fear or force he endeavors to rule the conscience and to secure homage to himself. To accomplish this, he works through both religious and secular authorities, moving them to the enforcement of human laws in defiance of the law of God.

Those who honor the Bible Sabbath will be denounced as enemies of law and order, as breaking down the moral restraints of society, causing anarchy and corruption, and calling down the judgments of God upon the earth. Their conscientious scruples will be pronounced obstinacy, stubbornness, and contempt of authority. They will be accused of disaffection toward the government. Ministers who deny the obligation of the divine law will present from the pulpit the duty of yielding obedience to the civil authorities as ordained of God. In legislative halls and courts of justice, commandment-keepers will be misrepresented and condemned. A false coloring will be given to their words; the worst construction will be put upon their motives.

Enacting a Law

As the Protestant churches reject the clear, scriptural arguments in defense of God's law, they will long to silence those whose faith they cannot overthrow by the Bible. Though they blind their own eyes to the fact, they are now adopting a course which will lead to the persecution of those who conscientiously refuse to do what the rest of the Christian world are doing, and acknowledge the claims of the papal sabbath. The dignitaries of church and state will unite to bribe, persuade, or compel all classes to honor the Sunday. The lack of divine authority will be supplied by oppressive enactments. Political corruption is destroying love of justice and regard for truth; and even in free America, rulers and legislators, in order to secure public favor, will yield to the popular demand for a law enforcing Sunday observance. Liberty of conscience, which has cost so great a sacrifice, will no longer be respected. In the soon-coming conflict we shall see exemplified the prophet's words: "The dragon was wroth with the woman, and went to make war with the remnant of her seed, which keep the commandments of God, and have the testimony of Jesus Christ." *Rev. 12:17.*

Marvelous in her shrewdness and cunning is the Roman Church. She can read what is to be. She bides her time, seeing that the Protestant churches are paying her homage in their acceptance of the false Sabbath, and that they are preparing to enforce it by the very means which she herself employed in bygone days. Those who reject the light of truth will yet seek the aid of this self-styled infallible power to exalt an institution that originated with her. How readily she will come to the help of Protestants in this work it is not difficult to conjecture. Who understands better than the papal leaders how to deal with those who are disobedient to the church?

Preparing for the End

The Roman Church, with all its ramifications throughout the world, forms one vast organization under the control, and designed to serve the interests of, the papal see. Its millions of communicants, in every country on the globe, are instructed to hold themselves as bound in allegiance to the pope. Whatever their nationality or their government, they are to regard the authority of the church as above all other. Though they may take the oath pledging their loyalty to the state, yet back of this lies the vow of obedience to Rome, absolving them from every pledge inimical to her interests.

The Warning Has Been Given

God's Word has given warning of the impending danger; let this be unheeded, and the Protestant world will learn what the purposes of Rome really are, only when it is too late to escape the snare. She is silently growing into power. Her doctrines are exerting their influence in legislative halls, in the churches, and in the hearts of men. She is piling up her lofty and massive structures, in the secret recesses of which her former persecutions will be repeated. Stealthily and unsuspectedly she is strengthening her forces to further her own ends when the time shall come for her to strike. All that she desires is vantage-ground, and this is already being given her. We shall soon see and shall feel what the purpose of the Roman element is. Whoever shall believe and obey the Word of God will thereby incur reproach and persecution.

To Destroy Faith in the Bible

The iniquity and spiritual darkness that prevailed under the supremacy of Rome were the inevitable result of her suppression of the Scriptures; but where is to be found the cause of the widespread infidelity, the rejection of the law of God, and the consequent corruption, under the full blaze of gospel light in an age of religious freedom? Now that Satan can no longer keep the world under his control by withholding the Scriptures, he resorts to other means to accomplish the same object. To destroy faith in the Bible serves his purpose as well as to destroy the Bible itself. By introducing the belief that God's law is not binding, he as effectually leads men to transgress as if they were wholly ignorant of its precepts. And now, as in former ages, he has worked through the church to further his designs.

The religious organizations of the day have refused to listen to unpopular truths plainly brought to view in the Scriptures; and, in combating them, they have adopted interpretations and taken positions which have sown broadcast the seeds of skepticism. Clinging to the papal error of natural immortality and man's consciousness in death, they have rejected the only defense against the delusions of Spiritualism. The doctrine of eternal torment has led many to disbelieve the Bible. And as the claims of the fourth commandment are urged upon the people, it is found that the observance of the seventh-day Sabbath is enjoined; and as the only way to free themselves from a duty which they are unwilling to perform, popular teachers declare that the law of God is no longer binding. Thus they cast away the law and the Sabbath together. As the work of Sabbath reform extends, this rejection of the divine law to avoid the claims of the fourth commandment will become almost universal. The teachings of religious leaders have opened the door to infidelity, to Spiritualism, and to contempt for God's holy law; and upon these leaders rests a fearful responsibility for the iniquity that exists in the Christian world.

Two Great Errors

Through the two great errors, the immortality of the soul and Sunday sacredness, Satan will bring the people under his deceptions. While the former lays the foundation of Spiritualism, the latter creates a bond of sympathy with Rome. The Protestants of the United States will be foremost in stretching their hands across the gulf to grasp the hand of Spiritualism; they will reach over the abyss to clasp hands with the Roman power; and under the influence of this threefold union, this country will follow in the steps of Rome in trampling on the rights of conscience.

The Basis of Genuine Revival

Many religious teachers assert that Christ by His death abolished the law, and men are henceforth free from its requirements. There are some who represent it as a grievous yoke; and, in contrast to the bondage of the law, they present the liberty to be enjoyed under the gospel.

But not so did prophets and apostles regard the holy law of God. Said David, "I will walk at liberty; for I seek Thy precepts." *Ps. 119:45*. The apostle James, who wrote after the death of Christ, refers to the decalogue as the "royal law," and the "perfect law of liberty." *James 2:8*; *1:25*. And the Revelator, half a century after the crucifixion, pronounces a blessing upon those "that do His commandments, that they may have right to the tree of life, and may enter in through the gates into the city." *Rev. 22:14.*

The claim that Christ by His death abolished His Father's law is without foundation. Had it been possible for the law to be changed or set aside, then Christ need not have died to save man from the penalty of sin. The death of Christ, so far from abolishing the law, proves that it is immutable. The Son of God came to "magnify the law, and make it honorable." *Isa. 42:21*. He said, "Think not that I am come to destroy the law"; "till heaven and earth pass, one jot or one tittle shall in nowise pass from the law." *Matt. 5:17-18.* And concerning Himself He declares, "I delight to do Thy will, O my God; yea, Thy law is within My heart." *Ps. 40:8.*

The First Step in Reconciliation

The first step in reconciliation to God is the conviction of sin. "Sin is the transgression of the law." "By the law is the knowledge of sin." *1 John 3:4; Rom. 3:20.* In order to see his guilt, the sinner must test his character by God's great standard of righteousness. It is a mirror which shows the perfection of a righteous character and enables him to discern the defects in his own.

The law reveals to man his sins, but it provides no remedy. While it promises life to the obedient, it declares that death is the portion of the transgressor. The gospel of Christ alone can free him from the condemnation or the defilement of sin. He must exercise repentance toward God, whose law has been transgressed and faith in Christ, his atoning sacrifice. Thus he obtains "remission of sins that are past," and becomes a partaker of the divine nature. He is a child of God, having received the spirit of adoption, whereby he cries, "Abba, Father!"

Free to Obey

Is he now free to transgress God's law? Says Paul: "Do we then make void the law through faith? God forbid; yea, we establish the law." "How shall we, that are dead to sin live any longer therein?" And John declares, "This is the love of God, that we keep His commandments: and His commandments are not grievous." *Romans 3:31; 6:2; 1 John*

5:3. In the new birth the heart is brought into harmony with God, as it is brought into accord with His law.

Satanic Delusions

As Spiritualism more closely imitates the nominal Christianity of the day, it has greater power to deceive and ensnare. Satan himself is converted after the modern order of things. He will appear in the character of an angel of light. Through the agency of Spiritualism, miracles will be wrought, the sick will be healed, and many undeniable wonders will be performed. And as the spirits will profess faith in the Bible and manifest respect for the institutions of the church, their work will be accepted as a manifestation of divine power.

How Satan Will Appear

Through Spiritualism, Satan appears as a benefactor of the race, healing the diseases of the people, and professing to present a new and more exalted system of religious faith; but at the same time he works as a destroyer. His temptations are leading multitudes to ruin. Intemperance dethrones reason; sensual indulgence, strife, and bloodshed follow.

The prophecy of Revelation 13 declares that the power represented by the beast with lamb-like horns shall cause "the earth and them which dwell therein" to worship the papacy—there symbolized by the beast "like unto a leopard." The beast with two horns is also to say "to them that dwell on the earth, that they should make an image to the beast"; and furthermore, it is to command all, "both small and great, rich and poor, free and bond," to receive "the mark of the beast." *Rev. 13:12, 2, 14, 16-17.*

A Restoration of Her Power

And prophecy foretells a restoration of her power. "I saw one of his heads as it were wounded to death; and his deadly wound was healed; and all the world wondered after the beast." *Rev. 13:3*. The infliction of the deadly wound points to the abolition of the papacy in 1798. After this, says the prophet, "His deadly wound was healed; and all the world wondered after the beast." Paul states plainly that the man of sin will continue until the second advent (*2 Thess. 2:8*). To the very close of time he will carry forward his work of deception. And the Revelator declares, also referring to the papacy, "All that dwell upon the earth shall worship him, whose names are not written in the book of life." *Rev. 13:8.* In both the Old and the New World, the papacy will receive homage in the honor paid to the Sunday institution, that rests solely upon the authority of the Roman Church.

Rapidly Being Fulfilled

In the events now taking place is seen a rapid advance toward the fulfillment of the prediction. With Protestant teachers there is the same claim of divine authority for Sunday-keeping, and the same lack of scriptural evidence, as with the papist leaders who fabricated miracles to supply the place of a command from God. The assertion that God's judgments are visited upon men for their violation of the Sunday-sabbath will be repeated; already it is beginning to be urged. And a movement to enforce Sunday observance is fast gaining ground.

Come Out of Her, My People

"I saw another angel come down from Heaven, having great power; and the earth was lightened with his glory. And he cried mightily with a strong voice, saying, Babylon the great is fallen, is fallen, and is become the habitation of devils, and the hold of every foul spirit, and a cage of every unclean and hateful bird." "And I heard another voice from Heaven, saying, Come out of her, my people, that ye be not partakers of her sins, and that ye receive not of her plagues." *Rev. 18:1, 2, 4.*

This Scripture points forward to a time when the announcement of the fall of Babylon, as made by the second angel of Revelation 14:8, is to be repeated, with the additional mention of the corruptions which have been entering the various organizations that constitute Babylon, since that message was first given, in the summer of 1844. A terrible condition of the religious world is here described. With every rejection of truth, the minds of the people will become darker, their hearts more stubborn, until they are entrenched in an infidel hardihood. In defiance of the warnings which God has given, they will continue to trample upon one of the precepts of the decalogue, until they are led to persecute those who hold it sacred.

Christ is set at naught in the contempt placed upon His Word and His people. As the teachings of Spiritualism are accepted by the churches, the restraint imposed upon the carnal heart is removed, and the profession of religion will become a cloak to conceal the basest iniquity. A belief in spiritual manifestations opens the door to seducing spirits and doctrines of devils, and thus the influence of evil angels will be felt in the churches.

The Final Warning

Of Babylon, at the time brought to view in this prophecy, it is declared, "Her sins have reached unto heaven, and God hath remembered her iniquities." *Rev. 18:5.* She has filled up the measure of her guilt, and destruction is about to fall upon her. But God still has a people in Babylon; and before the visitation of His judgments, these faithful ones must be called out, that they "partake not of her sins, and receive not of her plagues." Hence the movement symbolized by the angel coming down from Heaven, lightening the earth with his glory, and crying mightily with a strong voice, announcing the sins of Babylon. In connection with his message the call is heard, "Come out of her, My people." These announcements, uniting with the third angel's message, constitute the final warning to be given to the inhabitants of the earth.

A Clear-cut Issue

Fearful is the issue to which the world is to be brought. The powers of earth, uniting to war against the commandments of God, will decree that all, "both small and great, rich and poor, free and bond" (*Rev. 13:16*), shall conform to the customs of the church by the observance of the false sabbath. All who refuse compliance will be visited with civil penalties, and it will finally be declared that they are deserving of death. On the other hand, the law of God enjoining the Creator's rest-day demands obedience, and threatens wrath against all who transgress its precepts.

With the issue thus clearly brought before him, whoever shall trample upon God's law to obey a human enactment, receives the mark of the beast; he accepts the sign of allegiance to the power which he chooses to obey instead of God. The warning from Heaven is, "If any man worship the beast and his image, and receive his mark in his forehead, or in his hand, the same shall drink of the wine of the wrath of God, which is poured out without mixture into the cup of His indignation." *Rev. 14:9-10.*

A Clear-cut Test

The Sabbath will be the great test of loyalty; for it is the point of truth especially controverted. When the final test shall be brought to bear upon men, then the line of distinction will be drawn between those who serve God and those who serve Him not. While the observance of the false sabbath in compliance with the law of the State, contrary to the fourth commandment, will be an avowal of allegiance to a power that is in opposition to God; the keeping of the true Sabbath, in obedience to God's law, is an evidence of loyalty to the Creator. While one class, by accepting the sign of submission to earthly powers receive the mark of the beast, the other, choosing the token of allegiance to divine authority, receive the seal of God.

The first thirteen chapters of this book consisted of *STEPS TO CHRIST,* complete and unabridged. The last five chapters (chapters 14-18) of this book are from the heart of *GREAT CONTROVERSY* (60 pages from the full-sized 1888 edition of this book).

These are the sources for the five *Great Controversy* chapters:

CHAPTER 14 includes nearly all of *Great Controversy, chapter 29.*

CHAPTER 15 focuses on *Great Controversy, chapters 2 and 3,* but also includes portions of *chapters 1, 8, 16, and 26.*

CHAPTER 16 covers the greater part of *Great Controversy, chapter 25,* and much of *chapter 35.*

CHAPTER 17 has a large amount of material from the very important *chapters 33 and 34.*

CHAPTER 18 brings together the best of *chapters 27, 35, 36, 37, 38.*

THE PATHWAY TO HEAVEN — A STUDY GUIDE TO THIS BOOK

God's Plan for Your Life

In this book we have looked into the depths of the rich, enabling grace of Christ, given to forgive us and enable us, by faith in Christ, to obey the Law of God.

But now we want to understand that Law better. What is in the Ten Commandments; what do they mean to my life? Everything that God gives is perfect, and this is no exception. Here is God's beautiful standard for mankind: the Moral Law of God—the Ten Commandments. Trusting in Jesus, by His enabling grace, He will help you obey every part of it:

1- *"Thou shalt have no other gods before Me." Exodus 20:3.* Only God is entitled to our supreme reverence and worship. Nothing else is to have first place in our affections or service. Anything else that lessens our love for, and obedience, to God—becomes a god more important to us than our heavenly Father.

2- *"Thou shalt not make unto thee any graven image, or any likeness of any thing that is in heaven above, or that is in the earth beneath, or that is in the water under the earth: thou shalt not bow down thyself to them, nor serve them . ." Exodus 20:4-5.* We are not to worship God by images or similitudes. Representing Him by material objects lowers our conception of God, and can only result in the degradation of ourselves.

3- *"Thou shalt not take the name of the Lord thy God in vain, for the Lord will not hold him guiltless that taketh His name in vain." Exodus 20:7.* This commandment forbids false legal oaths and common swearing, and it also forbids using His name in a light or careless manner. He is holy and reverend (Psalm 119:19), and His faithful children will ever keep this in mind. His person and name should be thought of and spoken of with reverence and solemnity.

4- *"Remember the Sabbath day, to keep it holy. Six days shalt thou labor and do all thy work, but the seventh day is the Sabbath of the Lord thy God. In it thou shalt not do any work; thou, nor thy son, nor thy daughter, thy manservant, nor thy maidservant, nor thy cattle, nor thy stranger that is within thy gates. For in six days the Lord made heaven and earth, the sea, and all that in them is, and rested the seventh day. Wherefore, the Lord blessed the Sabbath day, and hallowed it." Exodus 20:8-11.* The importance of the Sabbath is here shown to date back to the Creation of the world, at which time God first gave the seventh-day Sabbath to mankind as a day set apart for divine worship.

"And on the seventh day God ended His work which He had made; and He rested on the seventh day from all His work which He had made. And God blessed the seventh day, and sanctified it, because that in it He had rested from all His work which God created and made." Genesis 2:2-3. After creating this world and everything in it in six days, our God set aside the seventh day as a day of rest. He rested on it, blessed it, and sanctified it,—that is, set it apart for our worship of Him.

The Sabbath is a sign that we love Him, obey Him, and are sanctified by Him. It is a sign of His creatorship and our sanctification and redemption. The Bible Sabbath is a sign that God is our Creator (Exodus 31:17), that He is the Lord our God (Ezekiel 20:20), and that He is the One who alone can sanctify us (Exodus 31:13). It is the sign or seal of the law. The only true Sabbath is the Bible Sabbath—the one given us in the Bible, the one kept on the day of the week that God set aside for us as the Sabbath day. This is the seventh day of the week, Saturday.

Astronomers tell us that, throughout history, time has never been lost. Historians tells us that the weekly cycle can be traced back thousands of years. The languages of man attest to the fact that the seventh day is the true Sabbath. (More information on this is available free from this publisher. Write for it.) But an astounding evidence of the true Sabbath is the Jewish people. Of all the ancient races of mankind, only the Jews remain a distinct people—in spite of the fact that they have not had a homeland for most of two thousand years. Through the Jews we can trace back to the Sabbath that Jesus (Luke 4:16), His disciples (Luke 23:56), and the apostles (Acts 13:14, 42; 16:13; 17:1-2) kept. Jesus said that, after His death, his followers must continue to keep the Sabbath (Matthew 24:20), and this they did (Luke 23:56, Acts 13:14, 42; 16:13; 17:1-2). But also, through the Jews, we can trace the weekly cycle and the true Sabbath all the way back to Moses, at which time God gave the Ten Commandments in written form.

There is no doubt as to which day is the true Sabbath, and there is no doubt that God wants us to keep it. He never did away with His Moral Law, and we should not try to do so either. It is true that the "shadow laws" (Hebrews 10:1) were abolished at the cross. These were the laws of animal sacrifices in the earthly sanctuary. Type met antitype at the death of Christ on Calvary, and the statutes and ordinances of the ceremonial law were taken away at that time. But the Moral Law, contained in the Ten Commandments, is for us to reverently obey today. And we are to do it in the strength of Christ. By grace we are saved (delivered from sin), and by grace we are empowered to obey all that God has commanded in Holy Scripture.

What many do not understand is that "sin is the transgression of the law" (1 John 3:4), and that in order to be "saved from sin," we must be enabled to keep that law. And this can be done alone in the strength of Christ's enabling merits. Christ is our Righteousness: He alone is our Forgiver and our Enabler. Christ died to uphold the law and make it possible for you to obey it; He did not die, as some preach, in order to destroy the Moral Law! Christ did not die to destroy morality, but to guard and uphold it. He died to enable sinners to be forgiven and live godly, obedient lives (for godly living is what the Ten Commandments is all about). He did not die to destroy right living—Ten Commandment living,—and immortalize sin and take incorrigible sinners to heaven, there to defile it forever. But all this must be so if Christ died to do away with the Ten Commandments.

Jesus said in the Sermon on the Mount, "Think not that I am come to destroy the law, or the prophets. I am not come to destroy, but to fulfill. For verily I say unto you, Till heaven and earth pass, one jot or one tittle shall in no wise pass from the law, till all be fulfilled." Matthew 5:17-18. The original Greek word for "fulfill" here is *pleroo*, which means "to make full." It does not mean "to destroy or abolish." This same word is used in 1 John 1:4; John 15:11; 16:24; and 2 John 12, in the sense of "bringing to the fullest measure." Jesus said that He was sending the Holy Spirit "that your joy may be full." He did not mean that it would be abolished. This same Greek root word is found in "fulfill joy" (Philippians 2:2; John 17:13), "preach fully" (Colossians 1:25), and "obey fully" (2 Corinthians 10:6). Jesus concludes the above statement with a powerful warning not to disobey the Law of God: "Whosoever therefore shall break one of these least commandments, and shall teach men so, he shall be called the least in the kingdom of heaven; but whosoever shall do and teach them, the same shall be called great in the kingdom of heaven." *Matthew 5:19.*

The truth of the matter is that the seventh-day Sabbath is the only weekly sacred day given in the Bible. It was kept all through Bible times, and afterward for many centuries. But in the fourth century, A.D., the first Sunday Law was enacted, requiring the worship of God on Sunday, the first day of the week.

Sunday sacredness began in Persia about 200 years before the time of Christ. Worshipers of the Persian god, Mithra, gave Sunday its name, "The venerable day of the Sun," and worshiped on that day. Because Mithra was the sun god, they worshiped him by gathering on Sunday morning, and faced east—toward the sun—as they prayed. Very evangelistic, the Mithraites spread their faith all through the vast Roman Empire (Europe, the Near East, and North Africa). By the end of the third century, A.D., the majority of the people had been won to Mithraism or Christianity. Early in the fourth century, Constantine become emperor. Recognizing that the empire greatly needed strengthening, he counseled with the leaders of the Christian church at Rome—and, with them, developed the plan of uniting both religions into one—by having the people worship the God of the Christians, but do it on the sacred day of the Mithraites.

The plan of uniting the majority of the people into one religion succeeded dramatically as a single State Church was formed. Now everyone could easily become a Christian, and it was good politics to do so. Within a century the Christian churches in the cities were corrupted. It was really paganism that conquered, and the persecution of Bible-obeying Christians began in earnest. For centuries, Sabbathkeepers were proscribed, hunted, and slain.

That, in brief, is where Sundaykeeping came from, and why we have it today. Yet God predicted that this attempt would be made by the little horn power of Rome to change God's holy law: "And he shall speak great words against the most High, and shall wear out the saints of the most High, and think to change times and laws." *Daniel 7:25*. In one brief verse, we are warned of the amazing blasphemies, persecutions, martyrdoms, and efforts to change God's law—that would be attempted by this power. And time-laws are specifically mentioned. Any Catholic catechism will tell you that it was the Roman Catholic Church which changed the seventh-day Sabbath to Sunday. And, elsewhere in the catechism [Catholic lesson book], you will learn that the second commandment was taken out (forbidding image worship), the fourth was changed (removing the "seventh-day" from the Sabbath Commandment), and the tenth was then split in two (making two "covet commandments") in an effort to preserve the number ten.

God also predicted that people would arise who would repair the torn-out place in the law by again keeping the Sabbath Commandment. Carefully read Isaiah 58:12-14. And it was predicted that God's faithful believers in the last days would keep God's law. The persecution of the true church by the apostate church, during the Dark Ages, is predicted in Revelation 12:13-16, and then, in the last days, would come the remnant—or last part—of the true church: "And the dragon was wroth with the woman, and went to make war with the remnant of her seed, which keep the commandments of God, and have the testimony of Jesus Christ." *Revelation 12:17.*

Revelation 14:12 provides additional identification of this final group of faithful believers, just before the end of time: "Here is the patience of the saints: here are they that keep the commandments of God, and the faith of Jesus." By faith in Jesus they are enabled to obey the law of God. In the midst of a law-breaking generation, they will uphold obedience to God, and will stand faithful to the Ten Commandments.

Revelation 22:14 describes the entrance of His people into the City of God: "Blessed are they that do His commandments, that they may have right to the tree of life, and enter in through the gates into the city." Precious promise for those who now are ridiculed and derided for keeping God's commandments by faith in Christ.

But the future is bright for those who will stand loyal to God and His law—for that future is full of Jesus. Through eternal ages the people of God will worship Him on the Bible Sabbath: "For as the new heavens and the new earth, which I will make, shall remain before Me, saith the Lord, so shall your seed and your name remain. And it shall come to pass, that from one new moon to another, and from one Sabbath to another, shall all flesh come to worship before Me, saith the Lord." *Isaiah 66:22-23.*

5- *"Honor thy father and thy mother, that thy days may be long upon the land which the Lord thy God giveth thee." Exodus 20:12.* This is the fifth commandment. Parents are entitled to a degree of love and respect which is due to no other person. We are not to reject the rightful authority of our parents, and we are to give them love and tender care all through their lives, even to old age. We should also respect other authorities, as long as their rules do not conflict with the laws of God.

6- *"Thou shalt not kill." Exodus 20:13.* All acts of injustice that shorten life; the spirit of hatred and revenge, or the indulgence of any passion that leads to injurious acts toward others, or causes us to even wish them harm is a violation of the sixth commandment. It also includes a selfish neglect of caring for the needy and suffering, and all self-indulgence and intemperance that injures the health of ours elves or others.

7- *"Thou shalt not commit adultery." Exodus 20:14.* This commandment forbids not only impure actions, but also sensual thoughts and desires, and any practice which tends to excite them. Christ taught that the evil thought or look is as truly sin as is the unlawful action.

8- *"Thou shalt not steal." Exodus 20:15.* This commandment forbids manstealing, slave-dealing, and wars of conquest. It not only condemns theft and robbery, but demands strict integrity in the minutest details of life. It forbids overreaching in business and trade, and requires the payment of just debts or wages. No one is to advantage himself by the ignorance, weakness, or misfortune of another.

9- *"Thou shalt not bear false witness against thy neighbor." Exodus 20:16.* Included here is false speaking: every attempt or purpose to deceive another person. Falsehood is not only the act of misleading; it is also the intention to deceive. This can be done by a glance of the eye, a motion of the hand, or an expression of the face. All intentional over-statement, and even stating facts in such a manner as to mislead, is falsehood. Also included is every effort to injure the reputation of another by misrepresentation, evil surmising, slander, tale bearing, or intentional suppression of the truth.

10- *"Thou shalt not covet thy neighbor's house: Thou shalt not covet thy neighbor's wife, nor his manservant, nor his maidservant, nor his ox, nor his ass, nor anything that is thy neighbor's." Exodus 20:17.* The tenth commandment strikes at the very root of all sins, and prohibits the selfish desire, from which springs the sinful act. Covetousness lies at the heart of many of the iniquities of mankind.

The old song says, "Grace, grace, God's grace; grace greater than all our sins." And how truly great is the grace of God, for it is powerful enough to enable us to overcome all our sins and live a new life in Christ Jesus our Lord and Saviour. The law of God, written in our hearts, means obedience to it in the whole life. And this is not only what we want; it is also God's plan for us. As we live noble, godly lives, we are prepared for heaven, for we have heaven in our hearts.

— Includes material from Patriarchs and Prophets

Scripture Index

DESIRE OF AGES—The gripping story of Christ's life, from the manger to Calvary - and how it can help your life today. $16.95 ppd.

CHRIST'S OBJECT LESSONS—All the wonderful parables of Jesus, the Master Teacher. How to live better now - and how to prepare for an eternity with Him afterward. $12.95 ppd.

BEYOND PITCAIRN—A fascinating journey to other lands - that will finally bring you into the heart of one of history's strangest mysteries. $10.95 ppd.

MARK OF THE BEAST—Part 1 explains the Mark in Daniel 7 and Revelation 12-14. Dozens of facts and statements from historical sources. Part 2 is word-for-word from the heart of *Great Controversy*. $14.95 ppd.

NATIONAL SUNDAY LAW CRISIS—The history of the Sunday law movement in America - and where it is leading us. A powerful book, with a full chapter on the implications of the Genocide Treaty. $10.95 ppd.

If you have appreciated this book, you may desire further information about these subjects. For additional literature, please contact the address given below, or the publisher.